W9-AVT-424

ASTROLOGY

What's
Really in the
Stars

ASTROLOGY

J. V. STEWART, M. D.

 Prometheus Books

59 John Glenn Drive
Amherst, New York 14228-2197

Published 1996 by Prometheus Books

00 99 98 97 96   5 4 3 2 1

Library of Congress Cataloging-in-Publication Data

Stewart, J. V.
     Astrology : what's really in the stars / J. V. Stewart.
        p.   cm.
     Includes bibliographical references (p.   ) and index.
     ISBN 1–57392–077–0 (alk. paper)
     1. Astrology. 2. Astrology—History. I. Title.
BF1708.1.S73   1996
133.5—dc20   96–8675
                                                                  CIP

Printed in the United States of America on acid-free paper.

For Judith, Christopher, Holly, and Margaret

Contents

List of Illustrations   9

Acknowledgments   11

Introduction   13

PART ONE: THE ORIGINS OF ASTROLOGY

1. Mesopotamia (ca. 4000–1300 B.C.E.)   17

2. Assyrian Era (ca. 1300–600 B.C.E.)   40

3. New Babylonian Era (ca. 600–300 B.C.E.)   61

4. Astrology in Greece, Rome, and Hellenistic Egypt (ca. 600 B.C.E.–200 C.E.)   72

5. Ptolemy and the *Tetrabiblos*   88

Chronology of Origins of Astrology   104

PART TWO: ERRORS, DISCREPANCIES, AND QUESTIONS

6. Current Status   107

7. How Old Is Astrology?   110

8. Do the Sun, Moon, Planets,
   and Stars Affect Life on Earth?   116

9. Birth versus Conception, and Twins   122

10. Sign versus Constellation, and the Aquarian Age   125

11. Selective Memory, or the Versatile Human Mind   128

12. Questions   133

Conclusion   138

Bibliography   141

Index   153

List of Illustrations

1. The "Sorcerer" from the cave of Les Trois Frères
   (ca. 18,000 B.C.E.)   18
2. Map of the Ancient Near East   20
3. Calcite cylinder seal (3000 B.C.E.)   21
4. Greenstone cylinder seal, from Akkad (2300 B.C.E.)   23
5. Ziggurat at Ur   26
6. Ritual for the observance of eclipses   28
7. Divination by means of the liver   28
8. Divination by means of the intestines   29
9. Stone figure of a ram, from Uruk (ca. 3000 B.C.E.)   30
10. Stone figure of a bull, from Uruk (ca. 3000 B.C.E.)   31
11. Copper lion head, from Tell Al-Ubaid (2500 B.C.E.)   32
12. Omen report (ca. 1830 B.C.E.)   34
13. Model of sheep's liver, from Sippar (ca. 1800 B.C.E.)   35
14. Venus omens (Observations of the planet Venus)   36
15. Hittite text (thirteenth century B.C.E.)
    mentioning month of birth   37
16. Boundary stone (1100 B.C.E.)   38
17. Diverse biota on boundary stones   39

18. Sun god tablet, from Sippar (860 B.C.E.)   42
19. Omens from eclipse of the moon in Kislev   44
20. Omens from Cancer in lunar halo   45
21. Omens from thunder at month's end   46
22. Omens from evening first of Mercury in Taurus   47
23. Omens from an earthquake   48
24. Seven omen reports   49
25. Cuneiform planisphere (ca. 800 B.C.E.)   53
26. Mul-APIN tablet (ca. 700 B.C.E.)   54
27. Prehoroscopic astrology, from Uruk (fifth century B.C.E.) 64
28. Oldest horoscope, from Babylon (410 B.C.E.)   66
29. Babylonian horoscope, from Babylon (258 B.C.E.)   68
30. Babylonian horoscope, from Babylon (235 B.C.E.)   69
31. Babylonian horoscope, from Uruk (142 B.C.E.)   70
32. Graph/chronologies of early horoscopes   71
33. Greek papyrus horoscope (138 C.E.)   77
34. Greek horoscope (4 B.C.E.)   78
35. Greek horoscope (217 C.E.)   78
36. Greek horoscope (345 C.E.)   79
37. Astrological material by Vettius Valens (150 ca. C.E.)   86
38. Horoscope by Vettius Valens (106 C.E.)   87
39. Horoscope by Vettius Valens (116 C.E.)   87
40. Ptolemy   89
41. Portion of the *Tetrabiblos,* sixteenth-century manuscript 92
42. Contents of the *Tetrabiblos*   94
43. Dates of sun entering signs and constellations   126
44. P. T. Barnum Effect   129
45. Omen report (ca. 1000 B.C.E.)   131

Acknowledgments

To Ken Smith for his artistic work.

To Christopher Walker of the British Museum for his help with the chronology and translations of cuneiform tablets.

To Ivan Kelly for his help with portions of the manuscript.

If the sky is dark (on the first day) the year will be bad. If the sky is clear when the new moon appears, the year will be happy.

—Babylonian omen report (ca. 1900 B.C.E.)

We must be careful not to consider events that happen at the same time to have a cause-and-effect relationship. By this we mean that when two things happen at the same time, one of the events need not be the cause of the other.

—Donovan A. Johnson and William H. Glenn,
The World of Statistics (1961)

Introduction

We are all victims of mythology in one way or another, the inheritors of what man wishes to believe, regardless of whether it is true. Although much nonsense has been dispelled over the past century, as C. B. Clason points out astrology is still flourishing, a four-thousand-year-old monument to human credulity.

It is superfluous, I believe, to relate how important astrology has become today. Or rather, re-become. It has had several high periods, and a few lows, in its life. Astrology is, and should be treated as, a religion. After acquiring a smattering of the lore, the tendency is to become more of a believer rather than less of one. The maxims and dogmas of astrology have the added benefit of astronomical facts, which few religions possess. The human spirit wishes to belong. It is much simpler to belong to a group (e.g., Aries) that you cannot do anything about. You cannot "give up" being an Aries. So, as seems to be the reasoning, you might as well accept it and look into it more.

Part One begins with the emergence of nomadic man who settled in lower Mesopotamia and ends with Ptolemy in Hellenistic Egypt, upon whose compilations, with surprisingly little modification, Western astrology is based. From Ptolemy to the present, astrology became a matter of interpretation, not innovation. Exceptions are, of course, discovery of the planets Uranus, Neptune, and Pluto. However, these bodies play questionable roles in horoscopic interpretation and their overall significance has been a subject of vacillation and debate among astrologers since their detection in the eighteenth, nineteenth, and twentieth centuries, respectively.

Part One traces the development of astrology from ancient times to Hellenism, showing how the ancient system evolved. With the early history, a concentrated effort has been made to get as close as possible to original source material. Though I take responsibility for translation errors, as well as for my own errors and omissions, all of the dates have been carefully researched.

Part Two indicates how, because of flaws in the framework of astrology, errors and discrepancies keep popping up creating problems. Using computerized statistical evidence has gradually exposed the randomness of astrological prediction. Unfortunately, statistical assailing has a tendency to create converts in defense of the subject, the argument being that pertinent information is missing. This book attempts to shore up the "pertinent ancient information" gap.

Of the enormous amount of material available on astrology, only a handful of books and papers deals with evaluation and criticism. The histories are written mostly by Assyriologists, historians of astronomy, and others who have taken the trouble to delve into the whys, wheres, and whos. From fragments of clay tablets, sometimes crumbling away before the eyes of the observer, an accurate chronology of events has gradually been put together.

Every dabbler and thus potential believer should acquaint himself with the early histories of O. Neugebauer, B. L. van der Waerden, and F. H. Cramer, as well as the critiques and statistical analyses of R. Culver, G. Dean, I. Kelly, and P. Ianna.

PART ONE

THE ORIGINS OF ASTROLOGY

1

Mesopotamia
(ca. 4000–1300 B.C.E.)

PROLOGUE

Recently, mitochondrial DNA studies have confirmed that modern man (*Homo sapiens sapiens*) originated in Africa about 150,000 years ago. Early man was a nomad and hunter, and because of harsh living conditions was mainly a cave dweller. Tools, carvings, engravings, sculpture, ivory beads and pendants, as well as human, horse, and mammoth drawings, have been found in sandstone rock shelters and caves during the Upper Paleolithic period (34,000 to 30,000 B.C.E.). Clay, ivory, and calcite figures of females, called Venuses, are frequently encountered. Cave art and rock figures are prominent between 22,000 and 18,000 B.C.E., and cave paintings are extensive from 18,000 to 11,000 B.C.E.

Mythological animals are frequently seen in the artwork of early *Homo sapiens sapiens*. Figures on cave walls of the Upper Paleolithic period in France (30,000 to 10,000 B.C.E.) depict bison-headed men and bisons with boars-heads, in addition to showing boars, oxen, bears, birds, deer, fish, cows, horses, ibexes (wild goats), lions, mammoths, and rhinoceroses.

17

Fig. 1: The Sorcerer from the cave of Les Trois Frères (ca. 18,000 B.C.E.). Neg. No. 329853 Photo. Logan, Courtesy Department Library Services, American Museum of Natural History.

Radiocarbon dating at 18,000 B.C.E. reveals one of man's first attempts at mythology, if we define mythology as an idea that is creative and imaginary: the "Sorcerer," a cave carving in the Grotte des Trois Frères, France, which shows a man disguised as an animal with antlers on his head, bear paws, the ears of a stag, and the tail of a horse (see figure 1). Various interpretations have been offered for this mythical creature, among them that this is a cave rite involved with magic, hunting, and fertility. Some feel it is shamanistic art (a *shaman* is a religious leader who communicates, often in a trance, with the spirit world on behalf of the community). Since the legs and feet are human, perhaps it is a disguised hunter creeping up on his quarry. Other human/animal *chimeras* (imaginary monsters) have been found, occasionally dancing. The *centaur,* or horse-man (the astrological sign of Sagittarius), is the derivative of such a creature.

Early Settlements

A primary requisite for the settling down of nomadic tribes was a trustworthy year-round supply of water, food, and building materials for homes. The plains and valleys between the Tigris and Euphrates rivers, and along the Nile River were good locations. Employing irrigation and the cultivation of crops on a large scale, man was no longer dependent upon the migration of animals for food.

The ancient area between the Tigris and Euphrates rivers is known by the Greek name *Mesopotamia,* meaning "between rivers." The nation of Iraq occupies most of this region today. By 7,000 B.C.E., the first settlements were being established. That there were similar beginnings in other parts of the world there can be little doubt, but they paralleled Mesopotamian development, being slightly less evolved.

The earliest community was at Muallafat in the northeast portion of Mesopotamia and the oldest city was Jarmo, dating to about 8000 B.C.E. By 6000 B.C.E., a canal irrigation system was created and pottery was made into a fine art. By 4300 B.C.E., farmers had begun to migrate from southwest Asia to the Lower Nile River valley and the first Egyptian civilizations were being established.

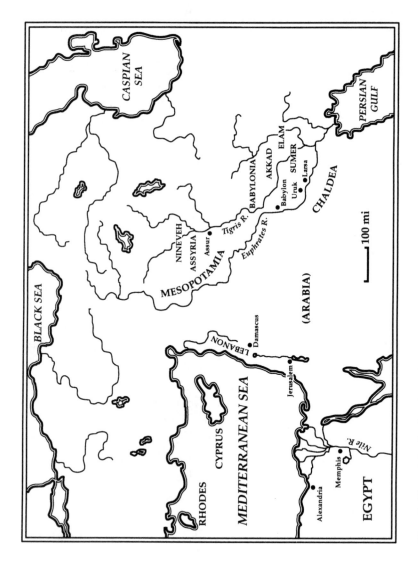

Fig. 2: Map of the Ancient Near East.

Fig. 3: Calcite cylinder seal (3000 B.C.E.). Copyright British Museum.

SUMER/AKKAD (CA. 4000–2000 B.C.E.)

The *Sumerians* were nomads who entered southern Mesopotamia from the east at the beginning of the fourth millennium (millennium = 1000 years; i.e., fourth millennium: 4000 to 3000 B.C.E.). Important Sumerian cities were Ur, Nippur, Kish, Larsa, and Uruk, which flourished about 3200 B.C.E. and at which writing was invented in 3300 B.C.E. In 3000 B.C.E., a people known as the *Akkadians*, speaking a different language (Semitic), migrated into the northern Tigris-Euphrates valley (see figure 2).

Considered gods or the homes of gods, the sun, the moon, and Venus (the most easily observed planet) were worshiped in early Sumer. Early evidence of this was on *cylinder seals*, prevalent several centuries before the invention of writing. A cylinder seal was a 2- to 3-inch stone cylinder with a decoration or personal engraving. When it was rolled over clay (or anything else), a raised pattern was made, impressing an individual's mark of authority on documents and property. Common motifs were the rayed disk of the sun, the crescent of the moon, and the eight-pointed star of Venus.

The calcite cylinder seal in figure 3 shows a temple facade with gatepost symbols of the Venus goddess Inanna. Two goats and sheep

approach. Around them are four spouted pots used for temple liba-
tions. Two scorpions and a snake are symbols of fertility.

The Sumerian cosmos, or universe, consisted of "heaven-earth"
(An-ki). The earth was a flat motionless disk, or perhaps a mountain. Heaven was a hollow space enclosed at the top and bottom by
a solid surface in the shape of a vault. The stars were nailed to the
archway over the earth. Across this archway moved the sun and
moon. Between heaven and earth was the air, or wind. Surrounding
the heaven-earth was a boundless, eternal sea. The gods of the
Sumerian pantheon were anthropomorphic. That is, they had
human forms and attributes. They were invisible and superhuman.
The following represents information written about 1750 B.C.E.:*

Creation of the Universe:

1. First was the primeval sea, existing eternally, and personi-
fied by the goddess Nammu. Nammu begot the cosmic mountain
consisting of heaven (An was the male heaven god) and earth (Ki
was the earth goddess) united, as well as the water god Enki.

2. The union of An and Ki produced the air god, Enlil, who
proceeded to separate the heaven-father An from the earth
mother, Ki.

3. Since all was now in total darkness, Enlil begot the moon
god, Nanna, the major astral deity of the Sumerians, who in turn
begot the sun god Utu and the goddess Inanna (who is later identified with the planet Venus).

Creation of Man:

1. Enlil now unites with his mother, Ki, and with the help of
Enki, produces plant and animal life.

2. Enki instructs his mother, Nammu, the goddess who begot
heaven, earth, and all other gods, how to fashion man. Man is the
eventual product of the combined efforts of Nammu, Ki, and Enki.

---

*Modified from S. Kramer, *Sumerian Mythology* (New York: Harper and Row, 1961).

Fig. 4: Greenstone cylinder seal, from Akkad (2300 B.C.E.). Copyright British Museum.

By the middle of the third millennium, hundreds of deities existed, at least in name. Many were duplicates. The more important in the Sumerian pantheon were the creation gods: An (the heaven god); Ki, or Ninhursag, or Ninmah, or Nintu (the earth goddess); Enki (the water god); and Enlil (the air god). Next in importance were the three astral deities: Nanna (the moon god), Utu (the sun god), and Inanna (the Venus goddess). There also were lesser gods and goddesses of such things as grain and cattle.

Each city-state had its own god. In 3000 B.C.E. at Uruk (Erech, or Warka), An (or Anu) was the supreme god of the Mesopotamian pantheon. Inanna, the goddess of love, was also worshiped. Later, the city-state Nippur, under the air god Enlil, became the spiritual center of the land. At Ur, Nanna or Sin, the moon god, was ruler. At Eridu, Enki ruled. Nergal (king of the nether world, later identified with the planet Saturn) was worshiped at Kutha. At Larsa and Sippar, Utu, the sun god, was supreme.

The Sumerian gods were assimilated by the Akkadians, and under other names took their places in the Akkadian pantheon. Utu, the sun god, became Shamash. Enki, the water god and god of wisdom, became Ea. Inanna, goddess of love, fertility, and war, became Ishtar. Nanna, the moon god, became Sin. Marduk, the principal god of Babylon, replaced Enlil (or Bel) of Nippur as the supreme god of the Akkadian and later Babylonian pantheon.

The greenstone cylinder seal from Akkad in figure 4 belongs to the scribe Adda. A hunting god with bow is present on the left. The goddess Ishtar, armed, winged, and holding a bunch of dates, is seen. The sun god Shamash is cutting his way through the mountains of the east. The water god Ea is accompanied by a bull. A bird is near a two-faced attendant.

The titles of gods, as well as their rulerships, changed frequently throughout the centuries depending on a variety of factors, among which was who conquered whom.

The Temple System

Priests who were able to communicate with the gods of the sun, the moon, and Venus were the first rulers. The priest had the multifaceted role of conducting religious business such as praying and offering animal sacrifices to the gods, as well as keeping farming and other records for the city-state. As time went on, the small temple expanded into a temple system with scribes, junior priests, agents, counselors, singers, musicians, weavers, pottery makers, bureaucrats, military people, and hangers-on. The temple system amassed large fortunes, owned much property and was the repository for cuneiform tablets. S. H. Hooke indicates that in a list of the temple staff of the goddess Baba in the time of Urukagina (ca. 2600 B.C.E.) 736 persons were enumerated, and later, in the great days of the Neo-Babylonian dynasty (first millennium), the staff of Marduk's temple numbered several thousand.

Eventually military leaders separated from temple leaders. A hodgepodge of rulers appeared. Some military leaders became kings. Priests, king-priests, junior priests, and priestesses emerged. The *baru*-priest, or seer, interpreted omens and dreams and observed the sky for warnings, mostly involving eclipses of the moon. He accompanied the king on campaigns and gave decisions about lucky and unlucky days to begin an attack. He also gave information about the future. The *baru*-priest could be called the first astrologer.

In order to communicate with gods, a mound representing a shrine was built from clay. Since clay crumbles, another mound was built on top of the first, and so on. As time went on, the mound increased in size. Eventually a multitiered structure, a temple-tower (*ziggurat*), was formed. It stood by the side of or on top of a temple, sometimes with two or more outside staircases with a shrine at the summit for animal sacrifices and to facilitate the gods' descent to earth. Later, the ziggurat was used by Babylonians and Assyrians to observe the heavens for omens and to map star formations. The oldest was constructed at Uruk, probably during the last half of the fourth millennium. Another large ziggurat was at Ur about 2100 B.C.E. (See figure 5.) The excavated remnant today is 260 by 175 feet wide. The most well known was at Babylon under King Nebuchadnezzar (606–562 B.C.E.). Known as the Tower of Babel, it was a reconstruction of an older ziggurat and was an observatory as well as a temple.

The *baru*-priest would retire to a special chamber in the temple known as *bit tamarti* (house of observation), or climb up to the flat roof of the campanile-type ziggurat, and observe the heavens all night long. Nowhere in the northern hemisphere must the sky have looked more beautiful on a clear night, or more ominous on a bad one, creating a wealth of speculation and fantasy.

The temple system developed rituals used to communicate with the gods. Divination was practiced by analyzing the intestines and livers of sacrificial sheep for omens. From the shape and quality of lobes of the liver, or appearance of loops of intestines, priests predicted good and bad dates and outcomes for wars, famines, and health of the king.

Later, omens from events of the day were recorded. Notations were kept about celestial occurrences, particularly phases of the moon and eclipses, the latter often portending catastrophes. The period of darkness in the lunar phase (*bubbulu*) was a time when evil spirits were particularly dangerous. Interpretation credibility was required, and priests became canny and a bit wily, since forecasting errors could result in banishment or death for the forecaster. Div-

Fig. 5: Ziggurat at Ur.

Above: Aerial view of the ziggurat. Copyright University of Pennsylvania Museum, Philadelphia (Neg. # NC35–9112).

Below: Restoration sketch of the ziggurat by Marjoris V. Duffell (1937). Copyright University of Pennsylvania Museum, Philadelphia (Neg. # S8–55876).

ination was molded into an art, with truth often moving into the background, not unlike the rituals of many of today's astrological practitioners and psychics.

Eclipse prediction was accomplished with correct mathematics, which later contributed to the early laws of astronomy. As the priest was praised for correctly forecasting an event, he would embellish his predictions with famines, plagues, and inundations. Monetary and other offerings from the people were encouraged.

The following are divination reports from the library of Ashubanipal from about 1200 B.C.E. to the Seleucid era. They are presented here to illustrate examples of priestly reporting. (See figures 6, 7, and 8.)

By the early second millennium, many of the animal and mythical creatures that were later to be incorporated into astronomical star patterns had already appeared in Paleolithic cave drawings and in the artwork and sculpture of Mesopotamia for several centuries. The bull was used as a common art theme from about the fourth millennium on in copper and bronze sculpture, and later on the sound boxes of lyres. The ram and the lion were on Uruk vases of the mid-third millennium. (See figures 9, 10, and 11.)

The water bearer, as the symbol of fertility, was present in second millennium statues. Sumerian artwork shows diverse biota such as lion-headed eagles, human-headed bulls, fish-men, winged-lions, centaur-lions, human-headed lions, geese, flies, gazelles, locusts, deer, monkeys, snakes, and scorpion-men. It is believed that many of these mythical creatures were the results of dreams and/or shamanistic rituals.

The astrological "elements" of earth, water, and air (fire was a later addition) were introduced by the Sumerians, as well as the religious mythology about the three most easily observed heavenly bodies: the sun, the moon, and Venus.

Science, including astronomy, did not exist in ancient Mesopotamia, nor did astrology. Early priests were concerned with correctly predicting the vagaries of the gods, such as eclipses, lightning, earthquakes, and famines, so that they, the priests, could retain power. In so doing, a calendar was created, as well as basic cycles of

This is that which to Sin during an eclipse he shall sing. In the gate of the house of the gods, and in the wide places, he shall place an altar (*garakku*).

Cedar, cypress, myrtle, good reed, mountain tamarisk, and a cedar *lutu*, upon the *garakku* thou shalt head up.

As the eclipse begins, the TU-E priest shall light the torch, and attach it to the *garakku*.

A dirge for the fields thou shalt intone; a dirge for the streams that the water shall not devastate, thou shalt intone.

As long as the eclipse lasts, the people of the land shall remove their headgear; they shall cover their heads with their garments.

That catastrophe, murder, rebellion, and the eclipse approach not unto Erech, Bit-resh, Eshgal the shrine of E-anna.

Seven workmen of the people of the country, the family, the dwelling, the river, their eyes, their hands and their feet, shall be anointed.

That catastrophe, murder, rebellion, and the eclipse shall not approach unto Erech, Bit-resh, Eshgal, the shrine of E-anna, and the houses of the gods of Tiranna, they shall cry aloud.

Until the eclipse is past, they shall shout. As soon as the moon appears from the eclipse, the fire upon the *garakku*, with the BI-MAT-NAM, thou shalt extinguish.

On the second day, the builder shall remove the *garakku*, including its ashes, and throw it into the river.

By Anu and Enlil conjure them. One magician on the right of the house, and a second on the left of the house, shall repeat the incantation Ud-uddu-a-mesh.

Fig. 6: Ritual for the observance of eclipses. From *Assyrian and Babylonian Literature: Selected Translations,* edited by R. Harper, D. Appleton & Co., 1901.

If on the surface to the right of the *ubanu* (the finger-shaped appendix of the liver), a finger is marked; the prince shall seize booty.

Fig. 7: Divination by means of the liver. From *Assyrian and Babylonian Literature: Selected Translations,* edited by R. Harper, D. Appleton & Co., 1901.

If the *tirani* (intestines) are like:

a scorpion; the temple will be rich; the weapon of the king will be true.

Gud-Gud-Na, fighting bull, and extends to the right; the forces of the king and his army will say: "a soldier of the king" and they shall march; he will not have a rival.

a human hand; there will be a famine in the land.

the heart of a fish; the king will be strong and he will not have a rival.

a decapitated bull, and extended beyond its size; there will be a famine of grain, straw, and vegetables in the land of the prince.

a star; the army of the prince will not have a rival.

Fig. 8: Divination by means of the intestines. From *Assyrian and Babylonian Literature: Selected Translations,* edited by R. Harper, D. Appleton & Co., 1901.

the sun, moon, planets, and stars. The year was divided into twelve months, based upon the approximate twelve yearly cycles of the moon. Attention was focused on events that could be successfully forecast mathematically.

OLD BABYLONIAN ERA (CA. 2000–1300 B.C.E.)

Hammurabi (1727–1685 B.C.E.) created the kingdom of Babylonia (the period of time from 1830 to 1530 B.C.E. is referred to as the Old Babylonian period). Hammurabi's legal decisions, known as the Code of Hammurabi, were collected and inscribed on a diorite stele (crystalline rock pillar) in the temple of Marduk. Under King Ammisaduqa (1581–1561 B.C.E.), one of the last of the Dynasty, omens were written about the appearance and disappearance of the planet Venus (Venus Tablets of Ammisaduqa).

The Hittites, a loose confederation of people from northeast Asia Minor and Syria, attempted an invasion of Babylonia in 1530 B.C.E. Babylon was sacked, but the Hittites were unable to hold the region. However, Babylonia was severely weakened.

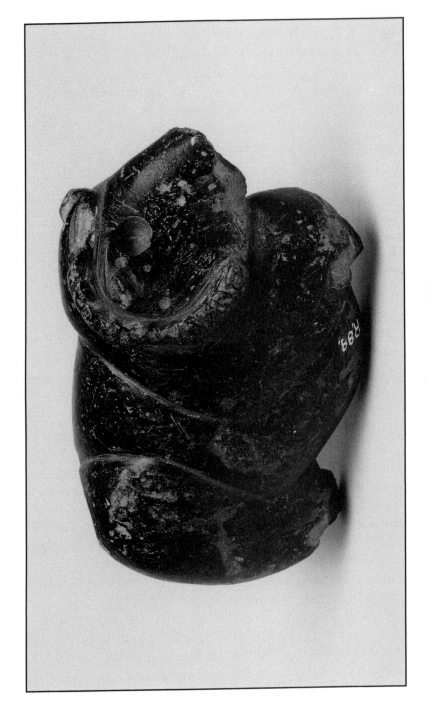

Fig. 9: Stone figure of a ram, from Uruk (ca. 3000 B.C.E.). Copyright British Museum.

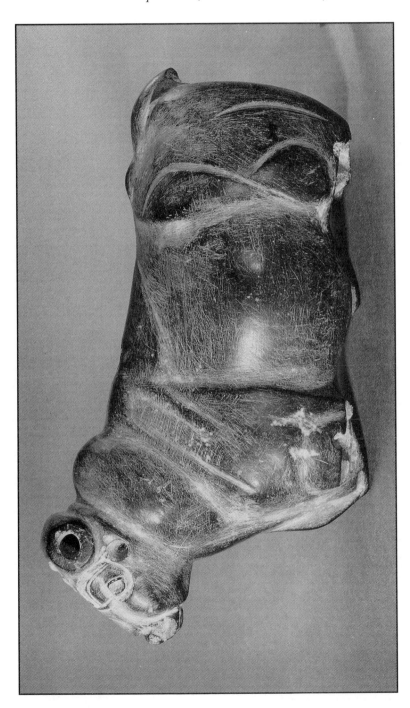

Fig. 10: Stone figure of a bull, from Uruk (ca. 3000 B.C.E.). Copyright British Museum.

Fig. 11: Copper lion head, from Tell Al-Ubaid (2500 B.C.E.). Copyright British Museum.

After the Hittite invasion attempt, Kassites from the eastern Zagros mountains conquered Babylonia and Assyria and remained for an unknown amount of time. The chronology here is weak, but according to clay tablets listing the reigns of kings, the Kassites seem to have been in power from 1530 to about 1275 B.C.E, when the Assyrians took Babylon.

The Development of Astrology

Pictures and symbols could, by pressing them into soft moist clay with a stylus or an instrument of wood, bone or metal, be preserved for an almost indefinite length of time. The script was given the name of *cuneiform* (Latin: wedge-shaped). The tablets, each about the size of a hand, were sun-dried or baked, being then virtually indestructible. However, clay drys quickly and each tablet had to be written at one sitting. This process was used for about 3 millennia. The sizes of the tablets were from $1 \times \frac{1}{2}$ inch to 15×9 inches. (After the fifth century B.C.E., Aramaic was inked with a brush onto cuneiform tablets. Aramaic displaced cuneiform in the Christian era. The last cuneiform tablet was written in 75 C.E. Papyrus continued to be used until about the tenth century C.E., when parchment, made from animal skin, gradually displaced it.)

One of the oldest astrological texts (see figure 12) comes from the Old Babylonian period.

Since the chief interest of Babylonia was the well-being of the country (not of the individual except for the king), predictions involved the weather, the harvest, drought, famine, war, peace, and the fates of kings. Regular occurrences of days, months, seasons, and years and agricultural life were important to the Babylonians and were dependent on the powerful moon and sun gods. Ishtar, goddess of the planet Venus and of Love, formed a trinity with the moon (Sin) and sun (Shamash).

Toward the end of the third and beginning of the second millennium, omen reports increased in appearances. A tablet from Sippar shows a model of a sheep's liver (probably used for instructing pupils). (See figure 13.)

> If the sky is dark (on the first day), the year will be bad.
>
> If the face of the sky is bright when the New Moon appears and (it is greeted) with joy, the year will be good.
>
> If the North Wind blows across the face of the sky before the New Moon, the corn will grow abundantly.
>
> If on the day of the crescent the Moon-God does not disappear quickly enough from the sky, "quaking" will come upon the Land.

Fig. 12: Omen report (ca. 1830 B.C.E.) From V. Sileiko, "Mondlaufprognosen aus der Zeit der ersten babylonischen Dynastie," *Comptes Rendus de L'Academie des Sciences de l'Union des Republiques Sovietiques Socialistes* (1927): 125.

A multitude of reports over several centuries, called Enuma Anu Enlil, were discovered in the library of Assurbanipal (669–630 B.C.E.) in Nineveh. Priests noted with accuracy the first and last appearance and disappearance, at sunrise and sunset, and the length of the appearance and disappearance, of the planet Venus, adding suitable predictions. These are the "Venus Omens" (see figure 14), contained in the sixty-third tablet of Enuma Anu Enlil. Most were written over a twenty-year period. The first report was probably written about 2300 B.C.E. The other three were likely written between 1581–1561 B.C.E.

Boundary stones made an appearance during the Kassite Period (1530–1275 B.C.E.), often showing the three main astral bodies. A boundary stone, or "kudurru," was a rounded stone monument in the field, about one and a half feet high, marking the limits of public or private property. It was engraved with pictures, symbols and script most often taking the form of a curse upon invaders of the domain. Doorsockets and steles (commemoratively inscribed stone monuments) were also engraved with similar formulae (see figures 16 and 17).

One of the earliest boundary stones is from the fourteenth century B.C.E., and shows (1) the crescent of Sin, (2) Shamash, and (3) the eight-pointed star of Ishtar. Also present are a scorpion, a shrine

Fig. 13: Model of sheep's liver, from Sippar (ca. 1800 B.C.E.). Copyright British Museum.

If Venus appears in the east in the month Airu
and the Great and Small Twins surround her,
all four of them, and she is dark, then will
the King of Elam fall sick and not remain alive.

(ca. 2300 B.C.E.)

If on the fifteenth day of the month Shabatu
Venus disappeared in the west, remaining absent in
the sky three days, and on the eighteenth day of the month
Shabatu Venus appeared in the east catastrophes
of kings; Adad will bring rains, Ea subterranean
waters; king will send greeting to king.

(1581–1561 B.C.E.)

If on the tenth day of Arahsamna Venus disappeared in
the east, remaining absent two months and six days in
the sky, and was seen on the sixteenth of Tebetu in the west, the
harvest of the land will be successful.

(1581–1561 B.C.E.)

If on the second day of Nisannu Venus appeared in the east,
distress will be in the land. Until the sixth of Kislimu,
she will stand in the east; on the seventh of Kislimu she
will disappear, and having remained about three months in the
sky, on the eighth of Adaru, Venus will shine forth in the west;
king will declare hostility against king.

(1581–1561 B.C.E.)

Fig. 14: Venus omens. Photograph copyright British Museum. Text from B. L. Van der Waerden, *Science Awakening II: The Birth of Astronomy,* Oxford University Press, 1974.

with a ram's head and a goatfish, twin lion-heads, a mace with a vulture head, a bird perched on a pole, a lightning fork placed on the back of a crouching ox, and a serpent.

In the thirteenth century B.C.E. is a prelude to natal, or genethliacal (the individual birth horoscope) astrology. It is a Hittite translation of a Babylonian omen text offering personal predictions according to the month in which a child is born (see figure 15).

The reader will note that the three astral bodies have acquired some significance. Particularly interesting is the fact that the love goddess, Ishtar, is represented by, or is, the planet Venus. Several hypotheses have been offered. Jastrow suggests that since the planet is above the horizon at sunrise (morning star) for eight months and five days, then after a three-month interval is above the horizon at sunset (evening star), this might have indicated the seasonal duality of the planet, and hence the two attributes as goddess of love and fertility, and of war.

Other than the sun and the moon, Venus is the brightest object in the sky. It is always near the sun. The sun and moon were both male gods. Because of the small, brightly glowing light of this "wandering star," the Babylonians identified it with the love goddess, shining forth with regularity.

If a child is born in the ninth month, he will die.
If a child is born in the twelfth month, he will grow old.

Fig. 15: The Hittite text (thirteenth century B.C.E.) mentioning month of birth. B. Meissner, "Ueber Genethlialogie bei den Babyloniern," *KLIO* 19 (1925): 432–34.

Fig. 16: Boundary stone (1100 B.C.E.). Copyright British Museum.

Fig. 17: Diverse biota on boundary stones. From W. J. Hinke, *A New Boundary Stone of Nebuchadnezzar I, from Nippur,* University of Pennsylvania, 1907. Photographs by Ferguson Photographics.

2

Assyrian Era
(ca. 1300–600 B.C.E.)

BRIEF HISTORY

In the thirteenth century B.C.E., Assyria began expanding. In 729 B.C.E., the Assyrians marched into Babylon and made Ashur leader of the gods, replacing Marduk. Sargon II came to the throne, and in 717 B.C.E. built Fort Sargon north of Nineveh, housing a large temple, ziggurat and library containing many tablets. Assurbanipal (669–630 B.C.E.) built a large library at Nineveh and began methodically accumulating all cuneiform literature in the Sumerian and Akkadian languages. Much of our knowledge of the development of ancient astronomy and astrology comes from this large collection.

THE EVOLUTION OF ASTROLOGY

The Assyrian pantheon remained essentially the same as the Babylonian, except that the god Ashur of the city of the same name along the west bank of the Tigris River replaced Marduk as chief of the gods. Ishtar became the second most important deity. Marduk absorbed the powers of Enlil, or Bel (later, the deity is spoken of as Bel-Marduk, and finally the prefix "Bel" is dropped altogether).

The tablet (see figure 18) from Sippar shows Shamash, the sun god, seated under an awning and holding a rod and ring symbolizing divine authority. His stool is supported by bull-men. Symbols of the sun, moon, and Venus are shown above him, plus another sun-symbol supported above him by an attendant of the god.

The first astrological predictions have to do with phases of the moon. Under the Assyrians, omens became profoundly important. They correlated them with the weather, earthquakes, and other catastrophes. The elements, in turn, affected crops of the city-states. Omens were directed toward favorable or unfavorable warring conditions for the state.

A problem that had plagued earlier cultures, an accurate and consistent calendar, was finally overcome in the eighth century B.C.E. (see later section). Star maps were accurately plotted and finally the zodiacal constellations (not the signs of the zodiac) were formed with a regularity of occurrence. These two factors, along with the development of accurate planetary tables, prefaced the invention of the horoscope in the fifth century B.C.E.

Planets, thought to be gods, possessed powers that were cyclical, awesome, and final. Exceptionally bright stars were allocated similar unique capabilities. The attitude of anthropomorphizing celestial bodies had not subsided, and would not subside into the Roman period.

OMEN ASTROLOGY

In the first millennium, omens had taken on prime importance in the affairs of the Assyrian state. Reports were presented to the court, or king, at various intervals by the priest-astronomer-astrologer. The astronomer-astrologer-priest who could foretell good things for the nation, or disasters and calamities for enemies, was a man whose words were regarded with reverence and respect.

Much of this enormous amount of omen material was compiled

Fig. 18: Sun god tablet, from Sippar (860 B.C.E.). Copyright British Museum.

by R. C. Thompson of the British Museum in the late nineteenth century: omens from the moon, omens from the sun, omens from the planets and stars, omens from thunder, omens from the moon's disappearance, omens from storms, omens from earthquakes, omens from eclipses, and omens from births. The reports compiled by Thompson were written by astronomer-astrologer scribes sent to various parts of the kingdom to gather information. The king was thus fairly well informed about the general course of events in his empire.

The thousands of omen tablets from the library of Assurbanipal deal with five main categories. They involve the country as a whole, crops, floods, the royal family, rebellion and the enemy. They do not involve the individual except for number five. It is felt that most were written about 1000 B.C.E., and some later. There are five main kinds of omens:

(1) *Enuma Anu Enlil,* or *celestial omens* (lunar, solar, planetary, and stellar).

(2) *Shumma Izbu,* or omens from monstrous births.

(3) Omens from the inspections of the internal organs of sacrificial sheep.

(4) *Shumma Alu Ina Mele Shakin,* or diverse omens about the behavior of animals, birds, insects, the digging of wells, and the location of cities.

(5) Physiognomic omens.

The emphasis here is with Enuma Anu Enlil, the celestial omens. Enuma Anu Enlil records ominous celestial events in connection with earthquakes, thunder, lightning, etc. and the effects on the country as a whole—crops, floods, the royal family, the nobility, rebellion, and enemies (see figures 19 to 24).

These examples give us an idea of the thinking of the Assyrian scribes. The majority of omens concern the king, crops, and weather phenomena. None mentions a birthday of an individual, including a king or prince.

If the moon disappears: evil will be established for the land.

If the moon is carried off at an inappropriate time: there will be an eclipse. The moon disappeared on the twenty-fourth day.

If the sun on the day of the moon's disappearance is surrounded by a halo: there will be an eclipse of Elam.

In Kislev (IX) there will be a watch for an eclipse. The halo which surrounded the sun, and the moon which disappeared, appeared for the sake of the eclipse watch of Kislev. The king should know it; let the king my lord be happy.

From Rasil the older, servant of the king.

Fig. 19: Omens from eclipse of the moon in Kislev. Photograph copyright British Museum. Text from H. Hunger, *Astrological Reports to Assyrian Kings,* Helsinki University Press, 1992.

[The moon] was surrounded by a halo, Cancer [sto]od in it. This is its interpretation:

[If the moon] is surrounded by a halo and Cancer stands in it: the king of Akkad will extend the life.

[If the moon] is surrounded by a halo and the north wind blows: the gods will raise [———, and] the gods will provide good fortune for the land.

[If the moon] is surrounded by [a halo] and it lingers on: givi[ng of the re]ign to [the king].

[If] there is fog [in the land]: plenty [for the people].

[If] there is continually fog [in] the land: the dynasty of the land will rule the world.

[If] there is continuous fog every day: business will become abundant.

[From] Sumaya.

Fig. 20: Omens from Cancer in lunar halo. Photograph copyright British Museum. Text from H. Hunger, *Astrological Reports to Assyrian Kings,* Helsinki University Press, 1992.

If on the day of disappearance of the moon Adad thunders: the harvest will prosper, business will be steady.

If it rains on the day of disappearance of the moon: the harvest will be brought in, and business will be steady.

May the lord of kings be everlasting!

From Asaredu.

Fig. 21: Omens from thunder at month's end. Photograph copyright British Museum. Text from H. Hunger, *Astrological Reports to Assyrian Kings,* Helsinki University Press, 1992.

If the star of Marduk becomes visible at the beginning of the year: that year his furrow will prosper. Mercury becomes visible in Nisan (I).

If a planet comes close to Aldebaran: the king of Elam will die.

If a strange star comes close to Enmesarra: people will spread; the land will become happy.

Mercury became visible in Taurus, it *reached* the Old Man.

If [a planet] becomes visible [in ——— rain]s and floods.

From [———].

Fig. 22: Omens from evening first of Mercury in Taurus. Photograph copyright British Museum. Text from H. Hunger, *Astrological Reports to Assyrian Kings,* Helsinki University Press, 1992.

> If the earth quakes in Nisan (I): the king's land will defect from him.
>
> If the earth quakes at night: worry for the land; abandonment of the land.
>
> From Aplaya.

Fig. 23: Omens from an earthquake. Photograph copyright British Museum. Text from H. Hunger, *Astrological Reports to Assyrian Kings,* Helsinki University Press, 1992.

When a halo surrounds the Moon and Regulus stands within it, women will bear male children.

From Nirgal-itir.

When Mars approaches Scorpio, the prince will die by a scorpion's sting, and his son after him will take the throne; the dwelling of the land ... the land another lord ... the boundary line of the land will not be secure.

No name.

When a foetus has eight legs and two tails, the prince of the kingdom will seize power. A certain butcher whose name is Uddanu has said, "When my sow littered, (a foetus) had eight legs and two tails, so I preserved it in brine, and put it in the house."

From Nirgal-itir.

... when Mars approaches Gemini, a king will die and there will be hostility.

Mercury is visible at sunrise in the precincts of Virgo. This is its interpretation. When Mercury approaches Spica, the crops of the land will prosper, the cattle will be numerous in the fields, the king will grow strong and will overcome (?) his enemies. Sesame and dates will prosper. ...

When Spica reaches Mars it will rain.

... When Venus appears in Virgo, rains in heaven, floods on (earth), the crops of Aharru will prosper; fallen ruins will be inhabited.

No name.

Fig. 24: Seven omen reports. From R. C. Thompson, *The Reports of the Magicians and Astrologers of Nineveh and Babylon,* Luzac and Company, 1900.

DAWN OF THE ZODIAC

In order to appreciate how it would be not to have a calendar, picture yourself as a priest in ancient Mesopotamia with farmers and others railing about crop and money problems, and nothing to guide your people into the seasons except perhaps the stars. So you, the priest, begin observing which bright stars or star patterns are overhead at night during each month when the gods (sun, moon and wandering stars) are in motion. Bright stars and star formations receive monthly names. Your competency as a forecaster of cycles and star patterns is challenged, and you spend a substantial amount of time acquiring knowledge of time and cycles in order to preserve your credibility, and perhaps your life.

Bright stars and star patterns that formed a belt through which the gods passed would be particularly important, and special names would be assigned to them. The path was the early zodiacal belt. Because the Babylonians used mostly animals (and some human and mythical creatures) to name these constellations, the Greeks referred to the belt as *zodiakos kyklos,* or "circle of animals."

The earliest star maps, about 1100 B.C.E., were lists of stars (astrolabes). Early tablets referred to the "stars in the path of the Moon." In the early first millennium, eighteen stars and constellations (including the twelve zodiacal constellations) as well as other astronomical features were described on three tablets known as mul.APIN. The twelve zodiacal constellations were finalized in the sixth century B.C.E. The signs of the zodiac (twelve equal 30-degree arcs) were not completed until the late fourth century B.C.E.

THE EARLY CALENDAR

The calculation of an accurate luni-solar time scheme was necessary for the development of horoscopic mechanics, because now celestial cycles could be plotted with consistent precision. The first calendars in Mesopotamia were lunar. That is, months were measured by noting one complete orbit of the moon around the earth, beginning shortly after sunset with the appearance of the first crescent. Since the Mesopotamians for several centuries attempted to correlate the lunar months with one solar year (the apparent revolution of the sun once around the earth, which cannot mathematically be done), it was necessary every few years to introduce a thirteenth month into the scheme.

It is interesting to note that the Egyptians, comparative latecomers to astronomy, used the solar year centuries before by associating the annual flooding of the Nile River with the rising of the star Sirius. P. W. Wilson says, "the trouble with the Babylonians was not lack of knowledge, it was a failure to act on knowledge acquired. They were conservatives and clung to lunar months. The Egyptians were progressives who had the courage to abandon it."

Under the reign of the King Nabonassar (747 B.C.E.), a lunisolar scheme was devised which equated 223 lunar cycles with a period of eighteen years (plus $11\frac{1}{3}$ days). Known as the Saros, it was the most accurate of earlier schemes and was introduced into consistent use by the fourth century B.C.E. The Greek astronomer-astrologer Ptolemy indicated that accurate records from the Mesopotamians were available only back to 747 B.C.E.

LISTS OF STARS (ASTROLABES)

The earliest schematic mapping of the heavens occurred in the mid-second millennium, and was the beginning of scientific astronomy. The oldest texts with systematic arrangements of stars and star clusters were *astrolabes*, or lists of stars. The scribes called these early lists "the three stars each." The oldest text was written in Ashur about 1100 B.C.E. and contains a list of thirty-six stars. Twelve stars describe a belt around the equator and are called the stars of Anu, the Sumerian heaven god. South of this are twelve stars of Ea, the Akkadian water god and god of wisdom, and north of this are the twelve stars of Enlil, the Sumerian air god and chief of the pantheon. The twelve stars of each belt were associated with the twelve months of the year. The official year varied widely because of the highly irregular association between lunar month, season, and the calendar.

The planisphere shown in figure 25 was like an astrolabe. The heavens were represented in eight segments which included drawings of the constellations.

mul.APIN

The cuneiform series mul.APIN (mul: star; apin: plough) named after its opening words, consists of three tablets, refining and continuing the development of astronomy and astrology. The oldest is from Ashur, about 687 B.C.E. The information may be older, however, probably between 1400 and 900 B.C.E. Mul.APIN was a compilation of all astronomical knowledge before 700 B.C.E. (one tablet has on the back the remark "Copy from Babylon").

The first tablet locates many stars, as did the astrolabes, and lists stars in the path of the moon. The second tablet deals with the sun, planets, and constellations in the path of the moon, the star Sirius, and the equinoxes and solstices, risings of some fixed stars, the planets and their periods, the four corners of the sky, the astronomical seasons, gnomon (early sundial) tables and omens connected with fixed stars and comets. Eighteen constellations are listed. Later combinations and deletions resulted in the twelve constellations of the zodiac (see figure 26).

The Gods who stand in the path of the Moon, and through whose domain the Moon each month moves and touches them:

1. MUL.MUL (zappu, the hair bush) = Pleiades
2. mul.GUD.AN.NA (the bull of Anu) = Taurus
3. mul.SIPA.ZI.AN.NA (Ann's true shepherd) = Orion
4. mul.SHU.GI (sibu, the old man or charioteer) = Perseus
5. mul.GAM (gamlu, siele sword) = Auriga
6. mul.MASH.TAB.BA.GAL.GAL (the great twins) = Gemini
7. mul.AL.LUL = Prokyon or Cancer
8. mul.UR.GU.LA (lion or lioness) = Leo
9. mul.AB.SIN (furrow) = Spica

Fig. 25: Cuneiform planisphere (ca. 800 B.C.E.). Copyright British Museum.

Fig. 26: Mul-APIN tablet (ca. 700 B.C.E.). Copyright British Museum.

10. mul.zi.ba.ni.tum (the scales) = Libra
11. mul.GIR.TAB (scorpion) = Scorpio
12. mul.PA.BIL.SAG (archer) = Sagittarius
13. mul.SUHUR.MASH (goatfish) = Capricornus
14. mul.GU.LA (great star or giant) = Aquarius
15. mul.zibbati.mesh (the tails) = Pisces
16. mul.SIM.MAH (the great swallow) = Piscis SW + e-Pegasi
17. mul.A-nu-ni-tum (the Goddess Anunitum) = Piscis NE + middle part of Andromeda
18. mul.LU.HUN.GA (agru, the hireling) = Aries*

THE ZODIACAL CONSTELLATIONS

By the sixth century B.C.E., the twelve zodiacal constellations had been mapped. A Cretan sage, Epimenides (600 B.C.E.), first mentions the constellation of Capricorn. A thirteenth constellation, Ophiuchus, the Serpent Bearer, which intrudes between Scorpio and Sagittarius, has never been incorporated into the plan, probably because of the consistent use of the number-12 lunar base.

Controversy has existed for a number of years about how the zodiacal constellations were named. The names were reminders of the seasons. The goal of Mesopotamian priests was to be able to recognize stars and star patterns in the night sky as reference points for (1) the seasons (and thus for a calendar) and (2) for the movements of wandering stars (gods, planets). Later, the Greeks created myths about the constellations which we know so well.

The Latin name with which we are familiar is listed first, then the Babylonian term and probable reason for the naming. At the end of each paragraph is a brief sketch of the Greek myth which evolved later in time:

1. *Aries* = LU.HUN.GA, meant "hireling," or "hired laborer." The constellation was renamed the Ram, probably by the Greeks.

*Adapted from B. L. Van der Waerden, "History of the Zodiac," *Archiv fuer Orient forschung* 216 (1953): 216–30.

Flocks were important to the shepherds and the ram was active in early spring. In Greek mythology, the golden fleece of the ram was the goal of Jason and the Argonauts.

2. *Taurus* = GU.AN.NA, or MUL, was "bull of heaven." The early constellation description around and before mul.APIN (687 B.C.E.) denotes Taurus equally well by MUL.MUL (Pleiades) or *is li-e* (Hyades—Aldebaran). Later just GUD.AN.NA (Taurus) was used. The bull symbolized the herds and the time for plowing. The Greeks embellished with a myth in which Zeus turns himself into a bull to kidnap Europa, and the forepart of a bull is placed in the sky.

3. *Gemini* = MAS.TAB.BA.GAL.GAL, or MASH, means "the great twins." The constellation contains the two bright stars Castor and Pollux, fairly close together. The Greeks told a story in which the brother Castor was killed in a battle. Pollux was griefstricken, and although immortal (being the son of Zeus), he prayed to have his immortality taken away unless he could share it with his twin. Zeus placed them together in the heavens.

4. *Cancer* = NANGAR, the crab. The idea of the crab may have arisen from the constellation once holding the summer solstice and the sun moving sideways for a few days, like a crab. In Greek mythology, while Hercules was burying the ninth head of the Hydra, the wife of Zeus, Hera, in a jealous snit, sent a crab to nip at his heels. Although crushed by Hercules, the crab was placed among the stars in gratitude by Hera.

5. *Leo* = UR.A, is a lion, or lioness. Originally the Babylonians saw two lions, the second including the southern part of Ursa Major. In the hot season in Mesopotamia, the lion was seen. In mythology, Hercules strangled a huge lion which had been ravaging the area, and wore the skin as protection against weapons of war.

6. *Virgo* = AB.SIN, originally meant "furrow" and referred to Spica, the principal star in the constellation. In mul.APIN, the star AB.SIN is the corn-ear of the goddess Shala. The idea of a goddess or virgin carrying an ear of corn appears in a line drawing of the Seleucid period. *Spica* is Latin for "ear of grain, or corn." Maidens and corn are seen in the fields at harvest time. In Greek mythology Virgo is identified with Astraea, daughter of Zeus and Themis, who left the

earth in disgust and was placed among the stars as Virgo. Sometimes she is represented with a pair of scales and a crown of stars.

7. *Libra* = *zi-ba-ni-tum*, means scales, for weighing after the harvest. It is the only nonliving sign of the zodiac. The scales may have referred to the equal day and night at the autumnal equinox. Earlier, Libra was the large claw of Scorpio.

8. *Scorpio* = GIR.TAB, means scorpion, which is in evidence in the fall. In a Greek account, Apollo sent a scorpion to kill Orion to protect his sister. Both Orion and Scorpio were then placed as far from each other as possible in the heavens.

9. *Sagittarius* = PA, is a centaur (half man and half horse) preparing to shoot an arrow. The origin is at least in the second millennium. A boundary stone from the Kassite period (ca. 1500–1200 B.C.E.) shows a winged centaur with two tails (one like a scorpion's), and two heads: a dog-head looking backwards and a man's head with a cap and mask, resembling a soldier's face shield. The face shield may have represented a fighting warrior on a horse. Seasonally, November and December are the hunting months.

10. *Capricorn* = SUHUR. In mul.APIN, SUHUR.MAS means goat-fish (SUHUR: goat, MAS: fish). The goat-fish is also seen in boundary stones from the Kassite period (see figure 17). The constellation is part of a western group involving water (i.e., Aquarius, the water carrier; Piscis Austrinis, the southern fish; Pisces, the fishes; Cetus, the whale). Later the fish was dropped, and the constellation is now "the horned goat." Since the goat climbs in the winter months, it is possible that the ancients related the climbing to the climbing of the sun in the sky after the winter solstice. The Greeks stated that the goat was actually Amaltheia, who was placed in the skies by Zeus out of gratitude for nourishment that she gave him when he was an infant.

11. *Aquarius* = GU, or GU.LA. The Mesopotamian meaning is unclear, but Aquarius represents a water-pouring god, with a fish involved (figure 17), or perhaps a water bearer, symbolizing the rainy season. Early artwork sometimes shows a boy or priest pouring water. The Greeks called the man Ganymede, one of the cupbearers to Zeus.

12. *Pisces* = *zib* is "band of fishes." In earlier cuneiform texts two

constellations are involved. The Greeks saw two fishes whose tails were tied together by a band. The constellation symbolizes fishing and the end of the rainy season. In Greek mythology, Aphrodite and Eros escaped from the monster Typhon by changing themselves into fish.

The only constellation that resembles its name is Scorpio, and then only with some imagination. It must be reiterated that the Sumerians, Akkadians, and Assyrians were acquainted for a long time with the ram, the bull, the twins, the crab, and fish (along the Ur and Eridu seacoasts), the lion, the virgin, the scales, the scorpion, the archer-warrior, the goat, and the water bearer. Much of the astrology of today is based on the simple relationship of star cluster to season. The reader might reflect, for a moment, upon the profound significance of this fact. This is the reason you are a Taurus, I a Capricorn.

THE PLANETS

Equally as or more important to the Assyrians than the zodiacal constellations were the placements in them of the five wandering gods, or planets. Each planet was considered a god, or the home of a god. The second tablet of the mul.APIN series discusses the relationships that the five planets and the moon have to the seasons. The names commonly identified with the planets were:

The Planets

Sun:	Shamash
Moon:	Sin
Venus:	Ishtar
Mercury:	Nebo, or Nabu
Mars:	Nergal
Saturn:	Ninurta
Jupiter:	Marduk

These names were eventually replaced by Greek deities, Roman names replaced the Greek, and English names sometimes replaced the Roman. Ishtar was originally the goddess of love, war, and fertility, later becoming only the goddess of love. Marduk was originally the god of the city of Babylon, then became the chief god of the Babylonian empire and eventually the chief of all the gods. Nebo was variously described as the scribe of the gods, the god of science and learning, the god of wisdom, and the messenger of the gods. Nergal was variously mentioned as the god of war and pestilence, the god of the underworld, and the god of hunting. Ninurta was a warrior of Bel (Bel, or Enlil, was also the lord of the lower world), a god of fertility, and a god of war.

According to Jastrow, Nergal (Mars) symbolized the destruction that accompanied war, and was not the strong champion who aided his subjects in the fight. Nergal was essentially a destroyer, at times the "god of fire," again "the raging king," the "violent one," and "the one who burns." (NOTE: the planet Mars is actually quite cold—below freezing—the mean temperature is –72° F.)

Since the planet Jupiter was thought to be the largest of the wandering stars, to it was ascribed the sphere of Marduk, chief of the gods. The period of revolution of Mercury is the shortest, thus the fastest, and to it was ascribed the sphere of Nebo. The reddish glow of Mars seemed best typified by the domain of Nergal. Venus, the bright wandering star with seasonal duality, was the domain of Ishtar. Finally, the small cold speck in the night sky of Saturn seemed best represented by Ninurta, god of the bleak lower world and of war. The earth was thought to be the motionless center of the universe and all revolved around it.

SUMMARY

Thus, all of the zodiacal constellations, as well as five of the planets, had been named and characterized by 700 B.C.E. The zodiacal signs, however, had not yet appeared. Some basic period-relations for the moon and the planets had been plotted. A consistent calendaric scheme (the Saros) came into full use by the fifth century B.C.E. A numerical methodology, which would later be applied to astronomical problems, was also developing. The crucial items necessary for the evolution of modern astrological mechanics that had not yet appeared by this time are: (1) the zodiacal signs consisting of twelve equal 30-degree arcs, (2) interpretations or predictions based upon the individual's birthday (natal or genethliacal astrology), and finally (3) the horoscope.

3

New Babylonian Era
(ca. 600–300 B.C.E.)

CHALDEAN ASTROLOGY

Under Nabopolassar, the Neo-Babylonian or Chaldean period began. The word *Chaldea,* from the Assyrian *Kaldu,* refers to southern Mesopotamia. Chaldean was used by the Greeks to denote Babylonian priests and scholars educated in literature, astronomy and astrology. Later Babylonian astrologers were known as magicians or Magi.

It is important to make the distinction between the historical Chaldeans—Mesopotamians who lived in southern Babylonia near the Persian Gulf—and the priests of Bel-Marduk, who made predictions based upon omens from internal organs of animals and astronomical events. The time frame of the Chaldean priests is roughly from the sixth century B.C.E. to about the second century C.E. Chaldean priests were the first to cast horoscopes.

The Greek geographer Strabo (63 B.C.E.–19 C.E.) describes the Chaldeans in his *Geography:*

In Babylon a settlement is set apart for the local philosophers, the Chaldaeans, as they are called, who are concerned mostly with astronomy; but some of them, who are not approved of by the others, profess to be genethlialogists (astrologers casting birth horoscopes). There is also a tribe of the Chaldaeans, and a territory inhabited by them, in the neighborhood of the Arabians and of the Persian Sea. . . . For example, some are called Orchenoi, others Borsippenoi, and several others by different names, as though divided into different sects which hold to various dogmas about the same subjects. And the mathematicians make mention of some of these men; as, for example, Kidenas and Naburanos and Sudines. Seleukos of Seleukeia is also a Chaldaean.

CHALDEAN ASTROLOGERS

Kiddinu (sometimes spelled Kidinnu, Kidenas, or Cidenas, ca. 340 B.C.E.) was a Babylonian astronomer/astrologer who practiced at Sippar along the Euphrates River southwest of Baghdad. Kiddinu methodically correctly plotted lunar and other cycles, including an accurate ecliptic period, setting the stage for the derivation of the precession of the equinoxes commonly attributed to Hipparchus.

Zeno of Citium (333–262 B.C.E.), a Greek philosopher who came to Athens from Cyprus, founded a school of philosophy called Stoicism which had as major tenets fatalism and predestination. Stoicism helped further astrology in the Hellenistic/Roman world.

Berossus (ca. 275 B.C.E.), a Babylonian priest of Bel (or Marduk), migrated to the Greek island of Cos, famous for its medical school, about 275 B.C.E. Berossus was an able historian and wrote three books in Greek (the *Babyloniaca*, or *Chaldaica*) describing the history and culture of Babylonia. He also founded a school of astronomy/astrology. Utilizing material from Kiddinu, he helped transmit Babylonian astronomy/astrology to the Greeks. Two students of Berossus, Antipatrus and Achinopoulus (ca. 258 B.C.E.), used the date of conception for horoscopes.

Sudines (ca. 220 B.C.E.), a Chaldean diviner, was court astrologer to Attalos I of Pergamum, not far from the island of Cos. He was also an authority on precious stones.

After Alexander the Great, Babylon and other Chaldean cities became religious centers. Omen reporting continued for several centuries, into the late Parthian period in the first century C.E. Divination by inspection of the liver and viscera of animals was regularly performed.

PREHOROSCOPIC ASTROLOGY

The following tablet from Uruk represents prehoroscopic data, mostly in the form of omens (see figure 27). It is one of the few pieces connecting omen astrology to Babylonian and Greek horoscopic astrology. Sachs dates it at about the fifth century B.C.E.

INVENTION OF THE ZODIAC

A critical step in the genesis of astrology was the invention of the zodiac, twelve signs of 30 degrees each. This must have taken place somewhere between 417 and 410 B.C.E. Astronomical diaries for 419 B.C.E. and 418 B.C.E. still use constellations, and the earliest known horoscope using signs is dated 410 B.C.E.

The final step was the creation of the *horoscope*. The oldest known horoscope (see figure 28), dated April 29, 410 B.C.E., comes from Babylon. It tells little except the astronomical data: the moon beneath the "horn" of Scorpio (the horn refers to the northern and southern pans of the constellation of Libra), Jupiter in Pisces, Venus in Taurus, Saturn in Cancer, Mars in Gemini, and Mercury invisible. The tiny nebulous statement "things will be good for you" offers little in the way of astrological prediction.

To date, sixteen Babylonian cuneiform horoscopes have been found, ranging in time from 410 to 68 B.C.E. Fifteen of the sixteen are from the Seleucid period, 280 to 68 B.C.E. Three of the fifteen are presented here (see figures 29, 30, and 31). The first and second

---

Fig. 27: Prehoroscopic astrology, from Uruk (ca. fifth century B.C.E.)

(Obverse)

The place of Aries: death of his family.
The place of Taurus: death in battle.
The place of Gemini: death in prison.

The place of Cancer: death in the ocean;
longevity. The place of Leo: he will
grow old, he will be wealthy; secondly,
the capture of his personal enemy.
The place of Virgo: he will be wealthy;
anger.

The place of Libra: good days; he will die
[at the age of?] forty years? The
place of Scorpius: death by rage [is?]
his death by fate. The place of
Sagittarius: death in the ocean.

The place of Capricorn: he will be poor,
he will be hysterical [?], he will grow
sick and die. The place of Aquarius:
[at the age of?] forty? years?, he will
have? sons; death by water. The
place of Pisces: [at the age of?] forty?
years?, he will die; distant days. . . .

If a child is born when the moon has come
forth, [then his life? will be] bright,
excellent, regular, and long.

If a child is born when Jupiter has come
forth, [then his life? will be] regular,
well; he will become rich, he will grow
old, [his] days will be long.

If a child is born when Venus has come
forth, [then his life? will be]
exceptionally? calm; wherever he may go,
it will be favorable; [his] days will be
long.

If a child is born when Mercury has come
forth, [then his life? will be] brave,
lordly; . . .

If a child is born when Mars has come
forth, [then] . . . , hot? temper?

If a child is born when Saturn has come
forth, [then his life? will be] dark,
obscure, sick, and constrained.

If a child is born when the moon is eclipsed,
[then his life? will be] dark, obscure, not
bright;

If a child is born when the sun is eclipsed,
[then] . . . , longevity.

(Reverse)

If a child is born when Jupiter comes forth
and Venus [had?] set, it will go
excellently with that man; his wife?
will leave, and . . .

If a child is born when Jupiter comes forth and
Mercury set, it will go excellently with that man;
his oldest son will die.

If a child is born when Jupiter comes forth
and Saturn set, it will go excellently
with that man; his personal enemy will die.

If a child is born when Jupiter comes forth
and Mars set, it will go excellently
with that man; he will see his personal
enemy in defeat[?].

If a child is born when Venus comes forth
and Jupiter had set, his wife will be
stronger than he.

If a child is born when Venus comes forth
and Saturn had set, his oldest son
will die.

If a child is born when Venus comes forth
and Mars had set, he will capture his
personal enemy.

If a child is born, and that day Jupiter
was visible for the first time after
conjunction, then. . . . If a child
is born, and that day Jupiter disappeared
[for the last time before conjunction],
then. . . .

If a child is born? when E bootis comes forth, he
will not have a son.

When B coronae borealis comes forth, he
will. . . . When B herculis comes forth, death
by a crane?

When u herculis comes forth, he will be poor.

When cygni comes forth, he will have the itch.
He will be deaf.

When n pegasi comes forth, he will die the
death of his fate.

When the constellation around v andromedae comes
forth, death by a snake.

When B persei comes forth, death by a weapon?

When a aurigae comes forth, he will be rich;
death by a weapon?

When a geminorum comes forth, death in prison?

When cancri comes forth, death by a weapon . . .

From A. Sachs, "Babylonian Horoscopes," *Journal of Cuneiform Studies* 6 (1952): 68–75.

Obverse

(Perhaps one line is missing.)

Month (?) Nisan (?), night (?) the (?) fourteenth (?) . . .

son of Shuma-usus, son of Shuma-iddina, descendant of Deke, was born

At that time the moon was below the "Horn" of the Scorpion.

Jupiter in Pisces, Venus

in Taurus, Saturn in Cancer,

Mars in Gemini. Mercury, which had set (for the last time), was (still) in[visible].

(Month) Nisan, the first (day of which followed the thirtieth day of the preceding month), (the

new crescent having been visible for) 28, [the duration of visibility of the moon after

sunrise on] the fourteen(?)th was 4,40(?);

the twenty-seventh was the-day-when-the-moon-appeared-for-the-last-time.

Reverse

(Beginning uninscribed).

(Things?) will (?) be good before you.

Month Du'uz, year 12,

[ye]ar (?) 8 . . .

[————]

(Rest of reverse, probably not more than one line, destroyed.)

Fig. 28: Oldest horoscope, from Babylon (410 B.C.E.). Photograph courtesy of the Visitors of the Ashmolean Museum, Oxford. Text from A. Sachs, "Babylonian Horoscopes," *Journal of Cuneiform Studies* 6 (1952): 54–57.

come from Babylon; the third from Uruk. The first horoscope offers no predictions, and combines conception and birth. The second offers several nebulous predictions. The third offers no predictions.

Only sixteen Babylonian horoscopes have been found out of some eighteen hundred astronomical tablets. With Greek horoscopes, the reverse occurs. About twenty astronomical tablets exist and ten times as many horoscopes have been found. It is interesting to note that the first Greek horoscope came into existence at about the same time that the last Babylonian horoscope was made, illustrating the significant role played by Babylonian astrology on Greek thought.

Figure 32 illustrates the respective chronologies of horoscopes.

QUALITIES OF SIGNS AND PLANETS

An interesting question, but one that remains speculative since tablets have not been recovered to indicate how the Babylonians developed the ideas, is to fathom how the qualities of planets in constellations and later in signs of the zodiac were derived. A plausible explanation, reinforced by Ptolemy, correlates obvious characteristics of the signs with obvious characteristics of the planets. For example, the sign of Leo the lion, in July-August, the hot summer season, goes well with the hottest planet, the sun. Wintry Saturn goes well with the winter signs Capricorn and Aquarius, and so on.

SUMMARY

To conclude, concomitant with the development of Babylonian astronomy and astrology was an evolution of Greek astronomy and astrology that began during the first part of the first millennium, as well as a similar growth of Egyptian astronomical/astrological ideas. While there was some exchange of ideas between the early Greeks and Babylonians, there seems not to have been much communication between Egypt and any other country prior to Alexander. Thus,

Obverse

Year 53 (of the Seleucid Era), intercalated (month Adar, on) the night
of the first, moon

[passed] below the star Barietis 2½ cubits (away).

The twelfth day: (vernal) equinox.

The first day: the moon . . . Pisces.

Reverse

Year 54 (of the Seleucid Era, month) Kislim, the first (day of which followed the thirtieth of the

preceding month, on) the night of the eighth.

in the beginning of the night, the moon was 1½ cubits below the star
(?) piscium,

the moon (having already) passed ½ cubit to the east.

The twentieth day: (winter) solstice.

The thirteenth day: the na of the moon was 11.

Upper Edge

At that time, Jupiter was in Capricorn, Venus in Scorpius,

—on the ninth (day), Mercury disappeared (for the last time) in the
east in Sagittarius—

Saturn and Mars in Libra

Commentary (Sachs, 52):

Kugler ingeniously recognized that this table represents a horoscope
combining conception and birth, despite the fact that the usual explicit
statement of the birth of a child is lacking.

Fig. 29: Babylonian horoscope, from Babylon (258 B.C.E.). Photograph copyright
British Museum. Text from A. Sachs, "Babylonian Horoscopes," *Journal of
Cuneiform Studies* 6 (1952): 58–60.

Obverse

    Year 77 (of the Seleucid Era, month) Siman, (from?) the fourth (day until? some? time?) in the

last part of the night (of?) the fifth (day),

Aristokrates was born.

That day: Moon in Leo. Sun in 12; 30° in Gemini

The moon set its face from the middle toward the top; (the relevant omen reads:) "If, from the

middle toward the top, it (i.e., the moon) sets its face, (there will ensue) destruction." Jupiter

. . . in 18° Sagittarius.

The place of Jupiter (means): (His life? will be) regular, well; he will become rich, he will

grow old, (his) days will be numerous (literally, long). Venus is 4° Taurus

The place of Venus (means): Wherever he may go, it will be favorable for him);

he will have sons and daughters. Mercury in Gemini,

(About four lines blank.)

Reverse

    with the sun. The place of Mercury (means): The brave one will be first in rank,

he will be more important than his brothers ———

Saturn: 6° Cancer. Mars: 24° Cancer . . .

the twenty-second and twenty-third of each month . . .

(Remainder of reverse uninscribed.)

Fig. 30: Babylonian horoscope, from Babylon (235 B.C.E.). From A. Sachs, "Babylonian Horoscopes." *Journal of Cuneiform Studies* 6 (1952): 60–61.

when we speak of a Babylonian genesis for astrology, this is true only up to about the sixth century B.C.E. Thereafter, modes of travel had developed to the point where exchange became inevitable. When we speak of the first horoscope being Babylonian, we should say that it was probably more Babylonian *than anything else*. With the later Babylonian horoscopes, more and more Hellenistic or Greek ideas permeated into and changed Babylonian astrology. It is this wealth of lore that was molded into substance by Ptolemy.

Obverse

[Year 1]69 (of the Seleucid Era), Demetrios (being king), month
Adar, (the first day of which

coincided with what would have been the) thirtieth (of the previous
month), the night of the sixth,

at the beginning of the night, the moon

was 1 cubit in advance (i.e., west of B tauri—

the sixth, in the morning, the child was born.

At that time, the moon was at the beginning of Gemini,

the sun in Pisces, Jupiter in Libra, Venus and Mars in Capricorn, Saturn in Leo.

That month, (the moon was) visible for the first time in the morning
after sunrise on the fourteenth;

Edge

last visibility of the moon (on the) twenty-seventh

Reverse

Year 170 (of the Seleucid Era,

month Nisan, fourth day; (vernal) equinox.

The child was born in the brilliant (?) house of Jupiter.

(Remainder of reverse uninscribed or destroyed.)

Fig. 31: Babylonian horoscope, from Uruk (142 B.C.E.). Photograph copyright British Museum. Text from A. Sachs, "Babylonian Horoscopes." *Journal of Cuneiform Studies* 6 (1952): 62–63.

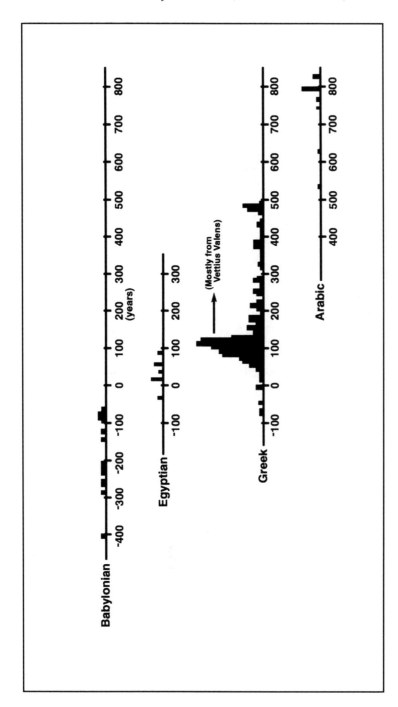

Fig. 32: Graph/chronologies of early horoscopes. Graph adapted form Otto Neugebauer and H. Van Hoesen, *Greek Horoscopes*, American Philosophical Society, 1959.

4

Astrology in Greece, Rome, and Hellenistic Egypt (600 B.C.E.–200 C.E.)

THE GREEKS

The sixth century saw the beginnings of Greek "philosophy" (love of wisdom) as well as the advent of many famous philosopher-scientists. Thales (625–547 B.C.E.) and Anaximander (610–547 B.C.E.), both of Miletus, began dealing with astronomy and logic, as did Pythagorus (580–500 B.C.E.). Philosophers were Socrates (469–399 B.C.E.), Plato (427–347 B.C.E.), and Aristotle (384–322 B.C.E.). Hippocrates (460–380 B.C.E.) on the island of Cos was the father of medicine. Euclid (ca. 295 B.C.E.) was an important mathematician. The fifth and fourth centuries B.C.E. were the Classical or Golden Age of Greece, and Athens became its bustling center.

By 350 B.C.E., Greek cities were declining. Alexander the Great succeeded in spreading Greek culture to other centers such as Alexandria and Antioch. *Hellenism*, referring to a Greek outlook and way of life, was created by allowing the network of Greek settlements and surrounding areas to develop a common culture. The Hellenistic period is from the time of the death of Alexander (323 B.C.E.) to the Roman conquest of the eastern Mediterranean in the middle of the second century B.C.E. Greek autonomy came to an end with the rise of Rome in the second century B.C.E. Greek scholasticism continued, however, and was incorporated into the Roman state, similar to the way in which Babylonian culture had been assimilated by the Greeks.

Greek Mythology

The planets were incorporated into Greek mythology. Hermes, son of Maia, was messenger of the gods, as well as the god of commerce, cunning, and invention. His home was the planet Mercury, which had the fastest of the planetary orbits. Aphrodite, daughter of Zeus and the Titan Dione, was the goddess of beauty and love. Her home was on the planet Venus. Ares, son of Zeus and Hera, was the god of war. His planet was Mars. The Greeks named the fifth planet (Jupiter) after Zeus. The sixth planet, Saturn, was associated with Cronus, symbolized by an old god (the planet was slow and obviously cold, since it was farthest away). Selene was goddess of the moon. Apollo was god of the sun, poetry, music, and beauty. The Greeks introduced a myriad of stories and poetry involving adventures of a multitude of gods and goddesses. Tales were modified and enlivened depending on the age, the city, and the lively imagination of the writer.

Greek Philosopher-Scientists

As far back as the sixth century B.C.E., the earth was thought to be round. Pythagoras (580–500 B.C.E.) argued that not only is the earth round, but the earth and planets revolve around a stationary sun. Pythagorus founded a religious, mystical, and philosophical school at Croton in southern Italy. The school survived into the next century and offered innovative ideas about mathematics and astronomy, including the Pythagorean theorem. The earth was a sphere. It was not the center of the universe but rather another celestial body moving in a circle, like all others. A "harmony of the spheres" existed. The energy for this was from Zeus. The Pythagoreans felt that the celestial bodies were divine. This divinity was acknowledged by Plato, somewhat by Aristotle and by scientists of later centuries, including Ptolemy.

Empedocles of Acragas in Sicily (493–433 B.C.E.) reintroduced the "elements" of earth, air, fire, and water, originally conceived by the Sumerians. Anaxagorus (500–428 B.C.E.), in contrast to Empedocles, felt that the elements were *not* earth, air, fire, and water, but rather units of smaller particles, and voiced the opinion that the sun was a fiery rock somewhat larger than the Peloponnesus (southern Greece). For this opinion, he was prosecuted and forced to leave Athens.

Plato, in the *Timaeus,* has Timaeus recite a monologue discussing the universe and reiterates Empedocles' idea of the four basic elements of earth, air, fire, and water. The celestial bodies are endowed with living, intelligent souls and move in various circles, some quickly and some slowly. Four kinds of living creatures populate the universe, corresponding to the four basic elements recognized in the cosmos: the divine kind of the heavens corresponding to fire, the winged kind to air, the watery kind to water, and the dryland creatures to earth.

In contrast to this thinking, another school existed in early Greece known as atomism, begun by Leucippus in the fifth century B.C.E. and continued by Democritus (460 B.C.E.). It was the forerunner of modern atomic theory and was roundly rejected by Plato and others. The story is told that Plato wanted to burn all of Democritus's works he could get hold of, but was dissuaded by two Pythagoreans.

Aristotle (384–322 B.C.E.) founded a breakaway school from the Academy in Athens called the Lyceum. He accepted the four "elements" of Empedocles, and added a fifth, "ether," which made up the heavens. He rejected atomism. Many of the concepts and ideas of the Lyceum were later transferred to the Museum at Alexandria during the last of the Hellenistic Period. Aristotle reinforced the Platonic doctrine of the divinity of heavenly bodies.

Eudoxus (400–347 B.C.E.) of Cnidus, a member of Plato's Academy, was the first Greek astronomer to crystallize mathematical astronomy. He was one of the first astronomers to integrate Greek and Babylonian astronomical ideas. Cicero remarked that Eudoxus wrote that, "not the least credence should be given to the Chaldeans in their predictions and assertions about the life of a man based on the day of his birth."

Aristarchus of Samos (310–230 B.C.E.), who was at Alexandria for a time, calculated distances of the moon and sun from earth, concluding that the sun was many times larger than the earth. Therefore, it seemed logical that the earth and planets may revolve around the sun and not the sun around the earth. For this heresy, Cleanthes the Stoic declared he should be indicted for impiety.

Hipparchus (190–126 B.C.E.) constructed the first extensive star catalogue (850 stars), dividing them into degrees of brightness, and devised the first practical method for determining the size and distance of the sun and moon. In addition, he elucidated the precession of the equinoxes. Hipparchus constructed an earth-centered (geocentric) system in which all of the heavenly bodies including the sun revolved around the earth, setting the stage for Ptolemy, who perpetuated the error. Almost nothing of Hipparchus's has survived except an early treatise, *Commentary on the Phaenomena of Eudoxus and Aratus.* Most of our knowledge of Hipparchus comes from Ptolemy.

Greek Astrologers

From about the fifth century B.C.E. to Ptolemy (ca. 150 C.E.), astrological information was transmitted from the Babylonians to the Greeks, who expanded and refined horoscopic astrology. Unfortunately the only records that have survived are fragments of tablets and papyri and comments from historians, such as Pliny and Plutarch.

Besides the Chaldeans Kiddinu, Berossus, and Sudines, discussed earlier, innovators of Hellenistic astrology were Critodemus (ca. 250 B.C.E.), Apollonius of Myndus (ca. 220 B.C.E.) and Epigenes of Byzantium (ca. 220 B.C.E.). The name "Petosiris/Nechepso" (ca. 150 B.C.E.), a possibly fictitious king/priest, appears from time to time in writings (astrologers often appear as shadowy figures in the literature, and time frames are often unreliable). Another name is Hermes Trismegistus, which is probably a Greek nonperson (the name actually means "thrice-greatest Mercury" in Greek), and the entity is sometimes referred to as the Hermetica. Both terms seem to be a scattered collection of philosophical and religious ideas from about the first to the third centuries C.E.

Poseidonius (135–51 B.C.E.), a Greek philosopher-scientist and prose writer, accurately calculated the size of the sun, and popularized astrology. Because of his stature as a writer and his friendship with Roman leaders, he was a major factor in the transmission and acceptance of astrology in Roman times and beyond.

Greek Horoscopes

Greek/Hellenistic horoscopes date from 62 B.C.E. to the seventh century C.E. (See figure 33.) The earliest Greek horoscope is for the coronation by Pompey of Antiochus I of Commagene in 62 B.C.E. The bulk of about 180 Greek horoscopes belong to the first five centuries C.E. One hundred thirty were produced by Vettius Valens. Nine Egyptian horoscopes belong to the interval 37 B.C.E. to 93 C.E. In general, the horoscopes say almost nothing. Instead of clay, later horoscopes (after about the year 1 C.E.) were written on papyri, ostraca, and graffiti (see figures 34, 35, and 36).

Summary of Greek Astronomy/Astrology

The Greeks, sadly, succeeded in presenting to the world many basic astronomical facts (of Aristarchus, Pytheas) which the world will not accept for fourteen centuries and then will have to rediscover (Copernicus). In the field of astrology, the horoscope, a product of late Babylonian and early Greek mathematics and astronomy, began to emerge.

A question that is sometimes posed is whether early Greek astronomers believed in astrology, or the power of divination according to the stars, and if so, why? The answer is that some Greeks were strong advocates of divination and others were not. In early times it was not inconsistent to be an astronomer as well as a "prognosticator of astronomy." The astronomers and mathematicians Pythagorus and Poseidonius were advocates of divination; Eudoxus was not.

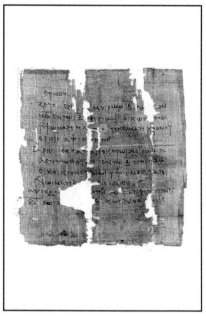

Fig. 33: Greek papyrus horoscope (138 C.E.). Copyright The British Library.

Year 27 of Caesar (Augustus)
Phaophi 5 according to the Augustan calendar
about the third hour of the day.
sun in Libra
moon in Pisces
Saturn in Taurus
Jupiter in Cancer
Mars in Virgo
[Venus in Scorpio]
[Mercury in Virgo]
[Scorpio is rising]
[Leo is at Midheaven]
[Taurus is then] setting.
Lower Midheaven Aquarius
There are dangers.
Take care for forty days
because of Mars.

Fig. 34: Greek horoscope (4 B.C.E.). From Otto Neugebauer and H. Van Hoesen, *Greek Horoscopes,* American Philosophical Society, 1959.

Didymos. Saturn in Libra
Jupiter (and) moon in Capricorn
Venus in Aries
sun in Taurus
Mercury (and) Mars in Gemini
Horoscopos in Leo

Fig. 35: Greek horoscope (217 C.E.). From Otto Neugebauer and H. Van Hoesen, *Greek Horoscopes,* American Philosophical Society, 1959.

In Libra (?)

With good fortune. Nativity of E[——]
Year 61, Epiphi third, eighth hour of day
Horoscopos (and) Jupiter in Libra
moon in Scorpio
Saturn in Aquarius
Mercury (and) Venus in Gemini
sun (and) Mars in Cancer
(The star) of Mars indeed approaching it (the sun) (at) 7 (degrees?)
with double prerogative, will cause
an anomaly. If no (other planet)
is there, since a (planet in) depression is not (effective)
it will effect nothing very bad;
but if Venus herself
intercepts it, it will even bring to the father
both patronage and success.

Fig. 36: Greek horoscope (345 C.E.). From Otto Neugebauer and H. Van Hoesen, *Greek Horoscopes,* American Philosophical Society, 1959.

ROMAN ASTROLOGY

Romans, particularly the nonnobility, began to be attracted to astrology after 250 B.C.E. For a price, astrologers would permit people to "outsmart the heavens." But Rome's conservative faction fought against religious penetration of Roman society by eastern cults, including Bacchus, Christianity, and Chaldean astrology. The Roman poet Ennius (239–169 B.C.E.) spoofed the "star gazers":

> But superstitious bards, soothsaying quacks, averse to work, or mad, or ruled by want, directing others how to go, and yet what road to take they do not know themselves; from those to whom they promised wealth they beg a drachme. From what they promised let them take their drachme as toll and pass the balance on.

Animal-named constellations were humorously called *Jove's animals*:

> He observes the signs of the astrologi what happens in the sky,
> when the goat or the scorpion or the name of some other animal
> of Jove rises. Not one of them pays attention to what lies before his
> feet. Raptly they gaze at the realms of heaven.

Some Greek philosophers visited Rome between 170 and 140
B.C.E. Opponents of astrology were Panaetius of Rhodes and the
astronomer Scylax, who repudiated the Chaldean method of fore-
telling the future. Carneades (214–129 B.C.E.), the more enthusias-
tically received of the group because of his gift as a speaker, also
opposed astrology. Carneades indicated:

(1) It is impossible to make precise observations of the heavens at
     the moment of birth (or conception).
(2) People born at the same moment under the same constella-
     tion have different destinies.
(3) People born neither at the same moment nor under the same
     constellation die at the same time.
(4) Animals too would be subject to the same fate as human
     beings born at the identical moment.
(5) The diversity of races, customs, and creeds regardless of
     whether or not people were born at the same moment under
     the same constellation, is incompatible with astrological tenets.

Because of the multitude of adverse problems concerning the in-
flux of diviners into Rome, an edict (Praetorian Edict of 139 B.C.E.) was
issued that expelled astrologers from the city. The edict listed two main
abuses for the expulsion order: (1) the fallaciousness of astrology as a
means of divination, and (2) the financial exploitation of gullible people by the unscrupulous practitioners of this pseudoscience.

The edict was poorly enforced, and by 100 B.C.E. astrologers
were visiting impoverished freemen and slaves. Astrology had an
ally in Poseidonius, who went to Rome in 87 B.C.E. Another advocate
was Publius Nigidius Figulus (99–44 B.C.E.), a senator who was also
an astrologer. In contrast, Marcus Tullius Cicero (106–43 B.C.E.),

orator, lawyer, consul of the Roman Republic, and writer, had strong objections to astrology. Among Cicero's works was the book *On Divination*. Beginning with a general statement, "My contention is that there is no divination," and borrowing from Carneades, he stated:

(1) Twins have different destinies although born under the same constellation.

(2) The sense of sight needed by the astrologers for observations of the heavens is fallible.

(3) Contrary to the tenets of fatalistic astrology, not all people born on earth under the same constellation have identical fates.

(4) If the stars, then surely winds and the weather in general also may influence a child at birth; i.e., not the stars alone.

(5) "The parental seed" also is an important factor in the future looks, habits, gifts, and outlook of a child. Hence the stars alone cannot determine such characteristics.

(6) Man's own exertion, or medical prowess often cure "natural defects" with which a child is born.

(7) Milieu and local traditions make men different, whether or not they are born under the same constellation.

(8) The assertion of age old observations providing the scientific proof of astrological claims is fraudulent.

Acceptance of Astrology by the Romans

Tiberius, Roman emperor from 14 C.E. to 37 C.E., had as friend and advisor the Alexandrian scholar and astrologer Thrasyllus, who arrived in Rome in 2 C.E. and later lived in Rhodes. The Latin poet *Marcus Manilius* (ca. 10 C.E.), which may have been a pen name for somebody else, was influenced by Thrasyllus. The *Astronomica* by Manilius was an unfinished astrological poem, of which five books survive. They were translated by the British classicist A. Housman in 1936, and, upon translation, are nearly undecipherable to Housman, as well as to myself. Dorotheus of Sidon (ca. 20 C.E.), who may have been an Egyptian, was an authority for Arabic astrologers. Fragments of a work called the *Pentateuch* have appeared from time to time.

In 33 B.C.E. and again in 11 C.E., astrologers were expelled from Rome. Between the death of Julius Caesar in 44 B.C.E. and the accession of Marcus Aurelius in 180 C.E., several such expulsion orders were recorded.

Court astrologers appeared. Babillus was astrological advisor to the Roman emperor Nero (37–68 C.E.). The Roman emperor Otho's (69 C.E.) favorite astrologer was Ptolemy Seleucus. Another astrologer was the Babylonian Teucrus in the first century, who emphasized *decans*,* and influenced Arabian astrology.

Hadrian, Roman emperor from 117 to 138, was himself a practitioner of astrology. His horoscope was retrieved by the astrologer Hephaestion of Thebes, who in the fourth century procured it with others from a collection compiled by the astrologer-physician Antigonus of Nicae. It is thought by many that the appointment of Ptolemy to the University at Alexandria was by way of Hadrian.

In the late second century, a comprehensive treatise against astrology was written by the Roman prose writer Sextus Empiricus (ca. 200), a portion of which is presented:

> If there are no gods, then there exists no divination. For this is the science which observes and interprets signs which are given to men by the gods. Nor could there be any prediction which is made by divine revelation, or through the stars. Nor by the inspection of entrails, or from dreams.

The last major Latin astrological work was the *Mathesis*, an astrological handbook written by a lawyer, Firmicus Maternus (ca. 337). In an odd contradiction to tradition, he writes:

> And no astrologer has ever been able to find out anything true about the fate of the emperor. For the emperor alone is not subject to the courses of the stars, and he is the only one whose fate the stars have no power to determine.

Decans, of late Egyptian origin, were divisions of each of the 30-degree astrological signs into thirds. Each 10-degree *decan* assumed an important role in horoscopic astrology.

Summary of Roman Astrology

The Romans were initially cautious of outside influences, including Chaldean, Greek, and later Christian cultures, as evidenced by frequent expulsions of foreigners. Since a respect for Hellenistic education existed, gradually other ideas gained footholds. At the time of Ptolemy (ca. 150), Egypt had been a Roman province for over a century, and Roman acceptance of astrology had an effect on Hellenistic astrology, particularly in Alexandria.

HELLENISTIC EGYPT

Alexandria, the main seaport along the Egyptian Mediterranean coast, was founded by Alexander the Great in 331 B.C.E. after its liberation from the Persian empire. Under Alexander's Macedonian general Ptolemy (Ptolemy I, or Ptolemy Soter), Alexandria became one of the more famous and successful of the Hellenistic capitals. A large university and library were established, and the university became the most famous institution of learning in the ancient world. A literary center, known as the Museum (Museion), was dedicated to the Muses. The essence of the Lyceum, begun by Aristotle, gradually shifted from Athens to Alexandria.

A tradition of famous scholars in Alexandria began with Strato and Euclid in 300 B.C.E., followed by Archimedes (ca. 250 B.C.E.), Eratosthenes (ca. 250 B.C.E.), Aristarchus of Samos (ca. 240 B.C.E.), Apollonius (ca. 200 B.C.E.), Aristarchus of Samothrace (ca. 170 B.C.E.), and Hipparchus (ca. 150 B.C.E.). The Septuagint, the oldest translation of the Old Testament by the Jews into Greek (about 250 B.C.E.), was written in Alexandria. Hellenistic scholars from many countries were invited to the library and museum.

The Museum at Alexandria contained 200,000 to 700,000 books (a book consisted of a papyrus roll wrapped around a wooden dowel, about ten inches in length, several inches to a foot in diameter, and was about twenty to thirty-five feet unrolled).

The populations, theologies, and cultures of Alexandria were Egyptian, Macedonian, Persian, Syrian, Jewish, Chaldean, Greek, and Roman. A common language was *koine,* a Greek dialect. About thirty sects existed. Gnosticism, a meld of Christian and Zoroastrian ideas, stressed knowledge of spiritual concepts and self-illumination. Serapis was a deity providing the Greek population with a patron god. Isis was an Egyptian goddess, introduced into Greece during the fourth century B.C.E. by expatriate Egyptians. Mithraism was a cult of the Indo-Persian sun god Mithras, introduced into the Hellenistic world in the second century B.C.E. Yahwists were Jews who believed in Yahweh as the single god.

Shortly before the death of Herod (4 B.C.E.), three hundred miles from Alexandria in a small village near Jerusalem, Jesus of Nazareth was born. Tradition relates that the Magi followed a bright star to Bethlehem. If the story is true, they were probably Persian astrologers. In 30 C.E., the year Alexandria became a Roman province, Jesus was crucified by the Romans. In 100 C.E., in Alexandria, Christianity was an obscure but rising cult.

When the Roman Empire gradually dwindled, Alexandria retained its status as a center of cultural activity. Christianity flourished up to about the third century, assisted by the Stoics. Alexandria declined and in 646 C.E. was conquered by the Arabs. The Arabs preserved many of the works of Euclid, Aristotle, Ptolemy, and others and translated them into Arabic. For several centuries the Arabs alone possessed the leading scientific material of the world.

As Alexandria began its decline late in the first century C.E., the scientific revolution that had flourished for two centuries (e.g., Euclid, Archimedes, Hipparchus) was dead. Robbins, translator of the *Tetrabiblos,* indicated, "by the second century A.D., the triumph of astrology was complete. With few exceptions, everyone, from emperor to the lowliest slave, believed in it, and having weathered the criticism of the New Academy, astrology was defended by the powerful Stoic sect." It was in this setting that Ptolemy and Vettius Valens emerged.

Vettius Valens

Vettius Valens (ca. 160 C.E.), one of the more notable Greek astrologers, was a contemporary of Ptolemy. As with Ptolemy, almost nothing is known of his life. He evidently maintained a school for prospective astrologers. Most of his work was done at Alexandria (confirmed by times and places of horoscopes, some done retrospectively).

According to Valens, each of the planets was assigned a role in the soul. In his work, the *Anthology*, he elucidated astrological theory using horoscope examples over the years 140 to 170 C.E. The *Anthology* consists of nine books, with titles "On the Hostile Places and Stars," "On the Critical Places According to the First Table of Critodemus," "On Violent Deaths with Examples," "Examples on Famous and Distinguished and on Obscure and Debased Nativities," and "Differently, on Critical Years, as Critodemus Takes the Start from the Moon."

Valens indicated he was not influenced by Ptolemy. "I decided to use Hipparchus for the sun, and Sudines and Kidynas and Apollonius for the moon—and moreover Apollonius for both kinds." (Apollonius was probably the astronomer/astrologer Apollinarius from the first century C.E.; Kidynas is another spelling for Kiddinu, or Cidenas. See figures 37, 38, and 39.)

Of the total 180 Greek or Hellenistic horoscopes in existence today, 130 were written by Valens, and are included in the *Anthology*. Neugebauer comments: "Without Vettius Valens we should have only five examples of horoscopes before A.D. 380." Astrologers contemporary with Valens were Antigonus of Nicaea (ca. 138 C.E.) and Critodemus, fifty years older than Valens, to whom he refers from time to time in the *Anthology*. Nothing is known of the life of Critodemus.

On the hostile places and stars.

It is necessary to investigate the hostile places and stars not only with respect to the other (planets) but also for the Horoscopos and sun and moon. Because these, also, when they come into diameter during their travel indicate crisis and death. Thus one must investigate, in the case of Saturn, the degrees at diameter, to which god the terms belong, as given in the table. And the person will die when Saturn is there or in the square of the Horoscopos or (in the places) with the same rising time, according to the combination of time in the squares of the Horoscopos or (in the places) with the same rising time. The same must be done also for the other stars because the rulers of the terms of the diametrically opposite decrees are hostile. If these planets come to the places (where the rulers of the diameter-terms are) or in (the places) with the same rising time, then they indicate destruction.

Thus let Saturn be in Cancer 21 degrees, terms of Venus. At diameter is Capricorn (21°), terms of Mars, who was in Taurus 27 degrees. He will die when Saturn is there. He died (when Saturn was) in Virgo because it is in its square, reckoned by degrees.

Jupiter in Scorpio 14 degrees, terms of Saturn. The fourteenth (degree) of Taurus is in the terms of Saturn. But it does not become hostile to itself. Now Leo has the same rising time as Scorpio and the fourteenth degree of Leo is in the terms of the sun. Thus Jupiter destroys when it comes to the places of the sun.

Mars in Taurus 27, terms of the sun. The same degrees of Scorpio are in the terms of the sun. But it does not become hostile to itself. Thus one must investigate the 27 degrees in Leo or in (the sign of) equal rising time (with ♉) which is Aquarius according to hourly distinctions; but the 27 (degrees) of Aquarius are in the terms of Venus. Thus he will die when Mars is in Scorpio or in Pisces, which are of equal rising time, or in their squares. If anyone reckons the 27 of Leo he will find the terms of Saturn. Saturn was in Cancer; thus he will die when Mars is in Cancer or in Sagittarius or their squares.

Venus in Scorpio 27 degrees, terms of the sun. The 27 degrees of Taurus at diameter are in the terms of the sun. But it does not become hostile to itself. Thus I investigate in (the sign of) equal rising time, Scorpio, the 27 (degrees); they are in the terms of Mercury. He will die when Venus is in Virgo where Mercury was; or in their squares. The same should be done with Mercury.

Also for illnesses it is necessary to investigate the diametrically opposite places and what planet is located in the hostile places and (the stars) which cause the crises of months, days, and hours according to the degree of the moon from which the opposing star is found.

Then from sun, moon, and Horoscopos the starter will be determined or else from the star found following the Horoscopos and so on in order to the other (stars) as they happen to be by sign and degree at time of birth; making the decision for (every period) of 10 years and 9 months.

Fig. 37: Astrological material by Vettius Valens (ca. 150 C.E.). From Otto Neugebauer and H. Van Hoesen, *Greek Horoscopes,* American Philosophical Society, 1959.

Sun (and) Saturn in Capricorn, moon in Scorpio, Jupiter in Leo, Mars in Pisces, Venus (and) Mercury in Aquarius, Horoscopos in Virgo, the Lot of Fortune in Scorpio, the Daimon in Cancer. Then in opposition to the Daimon, which forecasts the intellectual and the spiritual, was Saturn and he was in dominant aspect to the (preceding) full moon (in ♋) and to the phase at that time, and the ruler of the Lot of Fortune (♂) was in opposition to the Horoscopos. Thus this person had in the fated places injury and tender feet and most of all he was lunatic.

Fig. 38: Horoscope by Vettius Valens (106 c.e.). From Otto Neugebauer and H. Van Hoesen, *Greek Horoscopes,* American Philosophical Society, 1959.

Sun in Aquarius, moon in Virgo, Saturn in Taurus, Jupiter (and) Horoscopos in Gemini. Mars in Cancer, Venus in Pisces, Mercury in Capricorn, the Lot of Fortune in Capricorn, the Daimon in Scorpio. To these (lots) the maleficent (stars ♂ and ♄) were in opposition. This person was effeminate and he had unmentionable vices, for Capricorn is lascivious and its ruler (Saturn) was in Taurus, the sign (which indicates the kind of) weakness, and Scorpio indicates the kind of lasciviousness.

Fig. 39: Horoscope by Vettius Valens (116 c.e.). From Otto Neugebauer and H. Van Hoesen, *Greek Horoscopes,* American Philosophical Society, 1959.

5

Ptolemy and the *Tetrabiblos*

PTOLEMY

Ptolemy (Ptolemy of Alexandria, or Claudius Ptolemaeus, 100–170 C.E.), was not, strictly speaking, a Greek (see figure 40). He was also not, strictly speaking, even a Ptolemy. That is, he was not related to the original Macedonian general or the other Ptolemaic rulers of Egypt. He was an Egyptian astronomer, geographer, and mathematician who lived around Alexandria.

Little is known of his life, including whether or not he was involved with the museum or library at Alexandria. Knowledge of him has been pieced together from brief comments in his writings and offhand remarks from contemporaries. His birthplace was probably at Ptolemais Hermii, a Greek city in Upper Egypt. Roman citizenship was likely conferred on his ancestors. An occasional writer indicates that he was head librarian or superintendent of the Museum. This cannot be verified. The consensus is that he was probably appointed to a research post at the Museum. Ashmand indicated that in Whalley's translation of the *Tetrabiblos,* the Arabians report that "he was extremely abstemious, and rode much on horseback,"

Fig. 40: Ptolemy. Copyright Corbis-Bettman.

adding that although he was "spruce in apparel" yet his breath was not remarkable for an agreeable odor.

Using data derived from Hipparchus, Ptolemy mapped the positions of 1,028 stars (adding 172 to Hipparchus's star map), listed forty-eight constellations, more or less described the lines of longitude and latitude of the earth, and advanced the incorrect concept of an earth-centered solar system.

Ptolemy's most famous work is a thirteen-book mathematical astronomical work, the *Almagest,* or *Mathematike Syntaxis* (the Mathematical Composition). Hipparchus and Ptolemy believed that the earth was the stationary center of the universe and that all revolved around it; however, they found that from time to time the planets (not the sun and moon) appeared to be moving backwards for short periods of time in their orbits, then continued forward. An ingeniously complex scheme was devised to explain this apparent backward (retrograde) motion; the planets were thought to revolve around the earth in large orbits—but, each one also revolved in a smaller, faster circle (an epicycle) whose center was on the rim of the larger circle. In addition, there was an outer sphere carrying the stars around us. This is the Ptolemaic system, or less flatteringly, the Ptolemaic merry-go-round that survived for fourteen centuries.

Bartky observed, "we could stand at the center, then, as we watched the planets whirl around, and we could comprehend the Ptolemaic system. Then, as the spheres clanked on each other, we too would hear the 'Music of the Spheres'—a privilege that was reserved only for the gods and the extremely pious." Modern science has used this strange concept to show that this was the beginning of the fall of astrology, since it is totally incorrect. The problem is that it does not make any difference in the horoscopic system if it is or is not. As long as we are on earth, the "aspects" between celestial bodies are still the same.

Ptolemy's other works include a system of geography, the *Geography*; a work on optics, *Optics*; a musical work, *Harmonica*; and a large four-volume work on astrology, the *Mathematical Treatise in Four Books*, sometimes called *The Prognostics Addressed to Syrus*. (Syrus may have been a physician skilled in astrology. The *Almagest* was also dedicated to Syrus.) Later the work was called the *Tetrabiblos*, the name used today. Modern Western astrology is based, with surprisingly little modification, on Ptolemy's compilations and discussions in the *Tetrabiblos*.

Ptolemy mentions no contemporaries, such as Vettius Valens or the famous Greek physician Galen (130–200 C.E.) who was at the medical school at Alexandria during Ptolemy's time. Galen described Ptolemy as "a vitalist who attempts to transfer some basic concepts of vitalism to the dynamics of the heavens." It is not known how Ptolemy acquired the information used in the *Tetrabiblos*. However, in second-century Alexandria, the library had access to tablets and papyri on Chaldean and other theories on divination. Ptolemy may have received astrological information from Valens, although this is not known.

THE *TETRABIBLOS*

No original papyrus rolls of the works of Ptolemy exist. In fact, the originals of none of the ancients exist. All are copies and translations. The oldest translation of the *Tetrabiblos* is an Arabic version from the ninth century. Later Latin translations were the means by which Europe knew the *Tetrabiblos* (see figure 41). The English edition quoted in this text is a 1940 translation from the Greek by F. E. Robbins (see figure 42).*

In Book I, Ptolemy gives his rationale for pursuing astrology as a supplement to astronomy, commenting that:

> Some have brought about the belief that predictions depend on chance, which is incorrect. Others deceive the vulgar, because they are reputed to foretell many things, even those that cannot naturally be known beforehand. It is the same with philosophy—we need not abolish it because there are evident rascals among those that pretend to it.

---

*All excerpts are reprinted by permission of the publishers and Loeb Classical Library from Ptolemy, *Tetrabiblos*, translated by F. E. Robbins (Cambridge, Mass.: Harvard University Press, 1964).

Fig. 41: Portion of the *Tetrabiblos*, sixteenth-century manuscript. Copyright The British Library.

Ptolemy mentions that Mars and Saturn cause unfavorable events to happen, Jupiter and Venus favorable events, and Mercury either. The sun signs are characterized. Angles between planets are examined. The trine (sun, moon, or planets 120 degrees apart) and the sextile (60 degrees apart) are favorable; the square (90 degrees apart) and the opposition (180 degrees apart) unfavorable; the conjunction (the same degree plus or minus a few degrees on either side) may be either.

The five planets have a direct relationship to the various seasons of the year and each serves to rule the zodiacal sign in which the sun is placed along the ecliptic at that particular month.

The sign of Leo is allied with the hottest part of the year, late summer. To it is assigned the sun as ruler. It is, on this basis, a masculine sign and a fixed one. Midsummer is associated with Cancer, symbolizing feminine warmth. Opposite these signs are Aquarius and Capricorn, related to the coldness of the wintry months. Saturn is assigned as ruler of these signs because this planet is farthest removed from the sun and thus obviously colder.

The fire of spring is symbolized by Aries, and the dry, rotting, and burning season by Scorpio. Since Mars in the sky has a reddish hue, thus fiery, it is given the rulership of these two signs. The rulership of the temperate seasons of Sagittarius and Pisces is given to Jupiter, the largest planet. The warmth of fall and spring, which includes Libra and Taurus, seemed best typified in Venus.

Finally, the fast-moving planet Mercury may be either drying or humidifying because of its speed around the sun, and is related to seasons generally believed to be changeable, Gemini and Virgo.

Since the summer and winter solstices fall in the signs of Cancer and Capricorn, these are the solstitial signs. Aries and Libra, beginning on the equinoxes, are the *equinoctial* signs (these terms were later replaced by the term *cardinal*, which means the introduction to the four seasons). The *solid* (later called *fixed*) signs are Leo, Taurus, Scorpio, and Aquarius. The *bicorporeal* (later called mutable) signs are Gemini, Virgo, Sagittarius, and Pisces.

The *cardinal* signs introduce the seasons of spring, summer, fall, and winter. The *solid* signs were named because "when the sun is in them the moisture, heat, dryness, and cold of the seasons that begin

BOOK I

Introduction
That Knowledge by Astronomical
    Means is Attainable, and How Far
That it is also Beneficial
Of the Power of the Planets
Of Beneficent and Maleficent Planets
Of Masculine and Feminine Planets
Of Diurnal and Nocturnal Planets
Of the Power of the Aspects to the
    Sun
Of the Power of the Fixed Stars
Of the Effect of the Seasons and of
    the Four Angles
Of Solstitial, Equinoctial, Solid, and
    Bicorporeal Signs
Of Masculine and Feminine Signs
Of the Aspects of the Signs
Of Commanding and Obeying Signs
Of Signs which Behold each other
    and Signs of Equal Power
Of Disjunct Signs
Of the Houses of the Several Planets
Of the Triangles
Of Exaltations
Of the Disposition of Terms
According to the Chaldaeans
Of Places and Degrees
Of Faces, Chariots, and the Like
Of Applications and Separations and
    the Other Powers

BOOK III

Introduction
Of the Degree of the Horoscopic
    Point
The Subdivision of the Science of
    Nativities
Of Parents
Of Brothers and Sisters
Of Males and Females
Of Twins
Of Monsters
Of Children that are not Reared
Of Length of Life
Of Bodily Form and Temperament
Of Bodily Injuries and Diseases
Of the Quality of the Soul
Of Disease of the Soul

BOOK II

Introduction
Of the Characteristics of the Inhabi-
    tants of the General Climes
Of the Familiarities between Coun-
    tries and the Triplicities and Stars
Method of Making Particular Predic-
    tions
Of the Examination of the Countries
    Affected
Of the Time of the Predicted Events
Of the Class of those Affected
Of the Quality of the Predicted Event
Of the Colours of Eclipses, Comets,
    and the Like
Concerning the New Moon of the
    Year
Of the Nature of the Signs, Part by
    Park, and their Effect upon the
    Weather
Of the Investigation of Weather in
    Detail
Of the Significance of Atmospheric
    Signs

BOOK IV

Introduction
Of Material Fortune
Of the Fortune of Dignity
Of the Quality of Action
Of Marriage
Of Children
Of Friends and Enemies
Of Foreign Travel
Of the Quality of Death
Of the Division of Times
Index

Fig. 42: Contents of the *Tetrabiblos*. From Ptolemy, *Tetrabiblos,* translated by F. E. Robbins, Harvard University Press, 1964.

in the preceding signs touch us more firmly." The *bicorporeal* signs "are those which follow the fixed signs and are so-called because they are between the solid and the solstitial and equinoctial signs and share, as it were, at the end and the beginning, the natural properties of the two states of weather."

Signs may be favorable or unfavorable to one another. In the section "Of the Aspects of the Signs," Ptolemy comments:

> If we take the two fractions and the two superparticulars most important in music, and if the fractions one-half and one-third be applied to opposition, composed of two right angles, the half makes the quartile and the third the sextile and trine. of these aspects trine and sextile are called harmonious because they are composed of signs of the same kind, either entirely of feminine or entirely of masculine signs; while quartile and opposition are disharmonious because they are composed of signs of opposite kinds.

Regarding constellations and equinoxes (sidereal versus traditional astrology), Ptolemy indicates:

> The following, however, upon which it is worthwhile to dwell, we shall not pass by; namely, that it is reasonable to reckon the beginnings of the signs also from the equinoxes and solstices, partly because the writers make this quite clear, and particularly because from our previous demonstrations we observe that their natures, powers, familiarities take their cause from the solstitial and equinoctial starting places, and from no other source.

Book II examines predictions and the astrological signs of countries. Ptolemy comments that astrological events of countries and races take precedence over the individual.

> Prognostication by astronomical means is divided into two great and principal parts, and since the first and more universal is that which relates to whole races, countries, and cities, and the second and more specific is that which relates to individual men, which is called genethlialogical. We believe it fitting to treat first of the gen-

eral division, because such matters are naturally swayed by greater and more powerful causes than are particular events. The particular always falls under the general. It would by all means be necessary for those who propose an inquiry about a single individual long before to have comprehended the more general considerations.

Signs and planets ruling various countries are examined. Examples include:

> Of these same countries Britain, (Transalpine) Gaul, Germany, and Bastarnia are in closer familiarity with Aries and Mars. Therefore for the most part their inhabitants are fiercer, more headstrong, and bestial.

> The inhabitants of Hellas, Achaia, and Crete, however, have a familiarity with Virgo and Mercury, and are therefore better at reasoning, and fond of learning, and they exercise the soul in preference to the body.

Eclipses are analyzed. The human signs, Gemini, Virgo, Libra, Aquarius, and part of Sagittarius, cause events to happen primarily to humans, while the four-footed signs, Aries, Taurus, Leo, and the other half of Sagittarius, cause events to happen to four-footed animals. For example,

> The constellations both within and outside of the zodiac which are of human shape produce bodies which are harmonious of movement and well-proportioned; those however which are of other than human shape modify the bodily proportions to correspond to their own peculiarities, and after a fashion make the corresponding parts like their own, larger and smaller, or stronger and weaker, or more and less graceful. For example, Leo, Virgo, and Sagittarius make them larger; others, as Pisces, Cancer, and Capricorn, smaller. And again, as in the case of Aries, Taurus, and Leo, the upper and fore parts make them more robust and the lower and hind parts weaker.

The influence of planets on earth is explored. Saturn produces cold, floods, poverty, imprisonment, and death. Mars causes destruction through dryness, burning, and wars. The influence of comets and shooting stars on the weather is analyzed.

Book III relates to the individual. Conception and birth are examined. Conception time is preferred, birth being an accident. Conception time should be known, preferably by observation:

> In cases in which the very time of conception is known either by chance or by observation, it is more fitting that we should follow it in determining the special nature of body and soul.

The rising sign, moon's phases, and midheaven are examined. The influence of the father is shown through the sun and Saturn, the mother through the moon and Venus. Bodily form and temperament (the rising sign), injury, and disease are the result of favorable or unfavorable aspects of planets that rule certain parts of the body; for example,

> For, of the most important parts of the human body, Saturn is lord of the right ear, the spleen, the bladder, the phlegm, and the bones; Jupiter is lord of touch, the lungs, arteries, and semen.

The movements of planets and their effects on various nativities are examined; for example,

> Saturn, allied with Mars, in honorable positions makes his subjects neither good nor bad, industrious, outspoken, nuisances, cowardly braggarts, harsh in conduct, without pity, contemptuous, rough, contentious, rash, disorderly, deceitful, layers of ambushes, tenacious of anger, unmoved by pleading, courting the mob, tyrannical, grasping, haters of the citizenry, fond of strife, malignant, evil through and through, active, impatient, blustering, vulgar, boastful, injurious, unjust, not to be despised, haters of mankind, inflexible, unchangeable, busybodies, but at the same time adroit and practical, not to be overborn by rivals, and in general successful in achieving their ends. In the opposite positions

he makes his subjects robbers, pirates, adulterators, submissive to disgraceful treatment, takers of base profits, godless, without affection, insulting, crafty, thieves, perjurers, murderers, eaters of forbidden foods, evildoers, homicides, poisoners, impious, robbers of temples and of tombs, and utterly depraved.

If Mars or Venus, as well as the Sun and Moon are in masculine signs, the males become addicted to natural sexual intercourse, and are adulterous, insatiate, and ready on every occasion for base and lawless acts of sexual passion, while the females are lustful for unnatural congresses, cause inviting glances of the eye, and are what we call tribades; for they deal with females and perform the functions of males.

Book IV deals with occupation, material fortune, marriage, children, friends, enemies, foreign travel, death, and the "houses" of the zodiac. Ptolemy relates these to angles of planets; for example,

If Mercury and Mars together assume the lordship of action, they produce sculptors, armourers, makers of sacred monuments, modellers, wrestlers, physicians, surgeons, accusers, adulterers, evildoers, forgers.

EVALUATION OF THE *TETRABIBLOS*

The *Tetrabiblos* relegated other astrological works to historical interest only. Or, as Neugebauer points out, "the importance of a work can be measured by the number of previous publications it makes superfluous to read." Some modifications were made after Ptolemy, but the core of Western astrology was written in the *Tetrabiblos*.

The *Tetrabiblos* is a long composition with arduous sentences and is generally tedious and dry. However, sometimes the material draws a smile. The major problems, besides odd concepts, are unfinished and sometimes contradictory ideas. For example:

(1) The powers and characteristics of signs are taken from fixed stars in the constellations (sidereal astrology). However,

Ptolemy indicates that the "beginnings of the signs are to be taken from the equinoctial and solstitial starting-places, and from no other source."

In Ptolemy's time, a slight overlap existed between the signs and constellations. Today, because of the precession of the equinoxes, each sign has moved backward into the previous constellation. For example, a person with the sun in Aries has the constellation of Pisces overhead instead of Aries, and so on back around the zodiac.

But Ptolemy does not enlighten us. He was aware of the precession, since he was a follower of Hipparchus who had explained it three hundred years earlier. At the time of Hipparchus, the sun at the vernal equinox was 9 degrees in the constellation of Aries. In three hundred years (Ptolemy's time) the equinox had shifted about 5 degrees. We must be aware of the power of the fixed stars in the constellations, and yet the signs of the zodiac cannot be changed to correspond with the precession. How can this be done? It cannot, obviously.

So Ptolemy leaves one up in the air, as it were, dangling between constellation and sign. This, to me, is a major flaw of the *Tetrabiblos,* and is related to astronomical errors in the *Almagest.*

(2) A second problem involves the seasons. The seasons (solstitial and equinoctial starting places) vary according to latitude. Those described by Ptolemy and in Mesopotamian literature lie within a belt of about 6 degrees: from the ancient city of Barsa at the top of the Persian Gulf at $30\frac{1}{2}$ degrees northern latitude to Bosul, slightly above the now-extinct city of Nineveh at about $36\frac{1}{2}$ degrees northern latitude, in Iraq. North and south of these latitudes the seasonal changes, although at first subtle, nevertheless create changes on both sides of the equinoctial and solstitial points so that the seasons no longer correspond to the signs of a seasonal zodiac. The areas that differ include much of the world.

(3) A third problem involves the preference for conception-time over birth-time for casting of the horoscope. Conception-time cannot be known within less than a four- to five-day period (a fact not appreciated in Ptolemy's time). The horoscope would have meager meaning, since the rising sign changes every hour and a half.

(4) Another error involves signs of the same and different kinds. Ptolemy indicates that, "quartile and opposition are disharmonious because they are composed of signs of opposite kind" (e.g., masculine and feminine). This is *not* true with regard to the opposition. These are always of the same kind. For example, Gemini is opposite Sagittarius (two masculine signs); Virgo is opposite Pisces (two feminine signs), and so on.

(5) A last, rather odd comment is that a "general" horoscope (for a country or race of people) takes precedence over the individual nativity. This would negate about 95 percent of astrology.

PTOLEMY: AN EVALUATION

As mentioned earlier, little is known about Ptolemy, and his motives are difficult if not impossible to adequately assess. He seems to have had a substantial ego. Under his direction votive stelae were erected in the temple at Canopus, inscribed with his doctrines. There is no evidence that he ever practiced astrology. As far as is known he never cast a horoscope.

An uneasiness exists with the *Tetrabiblos*. O'Neil describes it as "reporting" rather than "constructing"; as, "received knowledge without any attempt to produce evidence even of an anecdotal sort." Farrington, who wrote the astrology section of the 1973 edition of the *Encyclopaedia Britannica,* indicates that Ptolemy "defends the system with a zeal beneath which the modern reader may perhaps detect evidence of embarrassment and even of bad faith; so compelling at this period was the astrological view," referring to the acceptance of astrology by the Roman Empire in the first and second centuries C.E.

Problems have arisen with Ptolemy's astronomical data. For several centuries, historians of astronomy have been uneasy about data in the *Almagest*. However, because of Ptolemy's stature in science, critics have looked the other way (Socrates would have scolded to press on for the truth, no matter where it led). As time went on, the suspicion was that numbers were doctored. Recent analyses concluded that numbers actually were skewed to fit hypotheses (in science more than just a misdemeanor and closer to a felony). In 1977, a geophysicist who researched Ptolemy's data concluded that *most* of his material was fraudulent. This was so disturbing that the geophysicist wrote a full-length book, *The Crime of Claudius Ptolemy*.

However, one may ask, why become upset with an ancient astronomer/astrologer and mathematician skewing a few numbers to fit a theory? The answer is that if he had pursued the truth, as Socrates cautioned, and had given correct numbers, a colleague or two may have been able to clarify the sun-centered solar system before Copernicus made sense out of it fourteen hundred years later.

Tools were at hand. Aristarchus had suggested a heliocentric system. Hipparchus had described the precession. Tools were available, but Ptolemy did not act. Why? We do not know. We know he was an avid supporter of Hipparchus. In fact, no tablets of Hipparchus have survived except through Ptolemy. Perhaps he was influenced politically. Negating a geocentric system and advocating a heliocentric system might have been politically risky.

How does the altering of astronomical data affect astrology? Celestial mechanics used by astrologers is based upon Ptolemy's data, much of which is incorrect. (For example, not dealing with the precession has created a continuing battle between sidereal and traditional astrologers.) Also, fraud has occurred, which makes motives questionable in other directions. What were Ptolemy's reasons for compiling the vast amount of astrological data from the Chaldeans? A sincere interest in the subject? Perhaps not.

Achievements

1. Wrote the earliest and most comprehensive treatise on Greek mathematical astronomy (the *Almagest*).

2. Compiled all astrological knowledge that existed up to that time (the *Tetrabiblos*).

3. Continued the work of Hipparchus, mapping the positions of 178 additional stars (plus Hipparchus's 850), and listed forty-eight constellations (based on Hipparchus).

4. Described instruments used for astronomical observations.

5. Accepted Hipparchus's correct estimate of the distance to the moon.

6. In *Optics* discussed the refraction of light.

7. In his book *Geography*, created maps, latitudes, and longitudes based on the marchings of the Roman legions through the then known world.

8. Wrote an innovative book on harmonics.

Errors

1. Perpetuated an incorrect theory of epicycles and an earth-centered (geocentric) universe, based upon the theories of Apollonius and Hipparchus. Discounted the correct sun-centered theory of Aristarchus.

2. Did not adequately utilize the precession of the equinoxes.

3. Manipulated and distorted data, thus confusing astronomy for fourteen centuries.

4. By accepting Poseidonius's estimate of the earth's size, (18,000 miles) rather than the correct one of Eratosthenes (25,000 miles), a significant error in maps, longitudes, and latitudes was made and perpetuated (when Columbus sailed to Asia, he thought it was a 3000-mile voyage instead of the correct 11,000-mile trip—which some say he would not have attempted).

5. Inadequately explained key features in the *Tetrabiblos*, such as the relationships of constellations, signs, and seasons.

AFTER PTOLEMY

An array of astrologers and philosopher/astrologers appears after Ptolemy and Valens. Porphyry (232–305) was a Greek Neoplatonist. Paul (ca. 378) of Alexandria composed a popular textbook used for a lecture course on astrology in the waning days of Alexandria. Others of whom little is known were Hephaestion of Thebes (ca. 380); Palchus (ca. 500), probably an Egyptian; Rhetorius (ca. 500); and

John Lydus (ca. 550), who practiced under Justinian I. The works of Ptolemy were continued, maintained, and commented on by the Alexandrian mathematician Pappus (260), the mathematician and astronomer Theon of Alexandria (364), and the Greek mathematician Proclus (460), who wrote a paraphrase of the *Tetrabiblos.*

After the fifth century C.E., astrological practice was curtailed until its revival in the eighth century when Hellenistic astrology was inherited by Islam. Albumasar (Abu Mashar, 787–886), a Muslim intellectual, expounded philosophical and historical justifications for astrology and helped introduce the lore to the Western world.

Chronology of Origins of Astrology

4000 B.C.E. to 2000 B.C.E. = Sumer/Akkad Period
Gods, goddesses of heaven, earth, water, air, sun, moon, Venus/ early calendar attempted

3300 B.C.E. = Writing invented, with pictographs of star, god, sky/first ziggurat
3000 B.C.E. = Akkadian migration into Sumer/cylinder seal depicting love goddess Inanna
2300 B.C.E. = Cylinder seal showing sun god Shamash, Ishtar, and water god Ea/earliest Venus omen report

2000 B.C.E. to 1300 B.C.E. = Old Babylonian Period

1900 B.C.E. to 1600 B.C.E. = Omen tablets
1700 B.C.E. = Hammurabi
1500s B.C.E. = Venus omens
1200 B.C.E. = Hittite tablet—prediction according to month of birth

1300 B.C.E. to 600 B.C.E. = Assyrian Period

1100 B.C.E. = Lists of stars (astrolabes)
1000 B.C.E. = Celestial omens (*Enuma Anu Enlil*)
600s B.C.E. = Accurate calendar developed/astronomical tablets (mul.APIN)
650 B.C.E. = Assurbanipal
Late 600s B.C.E. = All zodiacal constellations mapped

600 B.C.E. to 300 B.C.E. = New Babylonian Period

400s B.C.E. = Invention of zodiacal signs of thirty degrees each

Babylonian Horoscopes (total of sixteen in existence)

410 B.C.E. = Oldest known horoscope
68 B.C.E. = Last Babylonian horoscope

Greek (Hellenistic) Horoscopes (total of 180 in existence)

71 B.C.E. = Oldest Greek horoscope
510 C.E. = Last Greek horoscope

100 to 170 C.E. = Ptolemy
150 C.E. = *Tetrabiblos* written
160 C.E. = Vettius Valens
520 C.E. = Oldest Arabic horoscope

PART TWO

ERRORS, DISCREPANCIES, AND QUESTIONS

6

Current Status

Astrology is frequently depicted as an *a posteriori* concept, or reasoning from observed facts to valid premises which were laboriously worked out by the ancients. Instead, as we have seen, astrology is really *a priori* reasoning from faulty propositions lacking careful scrutiny.

Astrology is having a resurgence, not only because of mystical trends that ebb and flow over the years, but also because of the superabundance of astrological material easily accessible everywhere. Throughout its history, exacerbations and remissions are common, although remissions are not quite so common as exacerbations. Even though evidence is abundant showing flaws and fallacies of the art, astrology nevertheless appears to be marching along unscathed. Why? I discuss this with friends, and they nod, acknowledge my criticisms, then ask, "By the way, what's your sign?"

It is as if people are slightly brain-dead. As though one's sign is preordained and dissociated from one's body and reason. Most people are dabblers and feel it is simpler just to be a Leo, for example, rather than to seek evidence and evaluate available information. Relax and enjoy it is the reasoning. Besides, look at the positives about the sign. And even the negatives are not all that bad . . .

Computers and statistics, once thought to be the death rattle for horoscopic astrology, unfortunately have not shaken the faith of the believer. The suspicion is that statistics may be skewed. Even the dabbler is aware of this. The faith is being attacked and no amount of statistics will alter his conviction.

Scientists have been faced with a challenging dilemma. In 1941, B. J. Bok, an associate professor of astronomy at Harvard, in an article in the *Scientific Monthly,* spoke out against astrology. Later, in 1975, Bok organized the signing of a statement against astrology by 192 scientists, including nineteen Nobel laureates. However, sparse statistical evidence had been collected for and against astrology (both by scientists and astrologers). From a scientific standpoint, this was a weak thrust.

Fortunately, thanks to a handful of investigators, data now exist on nearly all facets of astrology, such as matching horoscopes with case histories, analyses of signs and planet locations, correlations with professions and other parameters, including predictions.

The overwhelming amount of evidence indicates that horoscopic astrology exhibits random, or chance, behavior. That is, if one were to select a concept out of thin air, or were to turn the horoscope upside down and make all Cancers Capricorns, a certain amount of positive results would still exist.

Culver and Ianna surveyed 3011 predictions made in astrology magazines from 1974–1979 and found only 11 percent were correct (at about the chance level), many of these being shrewd guesses, vagueness, or inside information. In 1977, Dean and Mather surveyed material from 1900 to 1976 in over seven hundred astrology books and three hundred scientific works that astrologers often use to reinforce the lore, including Bradley's work with rainfall and Jupiter, Nelson's work with radio propagation, Clark's matching tests, Jonas's method of sex determination, and the Mayo-White-Eysenck sun sign zigzag. None survived statistical analysis.

Dean in 1996 showed that the accuracy of astrologers' judgments (40 studies, 600 astrologers, 1092 charts) had a correlation of 0.05 (5 percent) or almost no correlation.

An interesting corollary presented itself regarding horoscopic interpretation, since disagreement exists among astrologers about how to interpret a chart. In fact, agreement is so poor it is nearly absent. Dean in 1996 showed that agreement between astrologers' interpretations using twenty-five studies, 488 astrologers, and 690 charts had a correlation of 0.10 (10 percent, or chance).

A dilemma, and one that astrologers often fall back on, is the fact that the horoscope generates an enormous amount of "possibilities." The birth chart utilizes about forty factors. I calculated the possibility of 583,200 major "aspects" in an average chart, omitting "progressions." There are, according to Argentine astrologer Carlos Baravelle, 10^{26} possible combinations of qualities in one chart. This monstrous figure means that no one could ever use it, let alone make sense out of it, even with a computer. (The computer is now an integral part of the business of astrology, along with software programs and data banks. A chart is now generated instantaneously. In 1991, astrology went on-line on the Internet.)

Dean in 1996 finally showed that the reliability of astrology is so low as to be almost nonexistent. Reliabilities down to 0.50 (50 percent) may be acceptable. Anything below 0.40 (40 percent) is generally regarded as too limited because the error rate is too high to justify use. For instance, the reliability of IQ tests is about 90 percent, personality inventories about 85 percent, palmistry is 11 percent, and astrology is last, at 10 percent (chance). In other words, most of the events attributed to astrology have nonastrological causes.

7

How Old Is Astrology?

The concept of star divination began in Sumer about 2300 B.C.E. with the reporting of the first Venus omens, and omen reporting flourished in the 1500s B.C.E. As mathematical astronomy evolved, reports merely became more sophisticated. As mentioned in chapter 1, about 1200 B.C.E., a tablet has been found displaying two small predictions according to the month of birth. The invention of the zodiac occurred between 418 B.C.E. and 410 B.C.E., and the earliest crude horoscope is dated 410 B.C.E.

Modern Western astrology (horoscopic astrology) developed as a synthesis of Chaldean lore and mathematical astronomy by the Greeks (Hellenistic astrology) in the 400s B.C.E. This synthesis was refined by Ptolemy and Vettius Valens in the second century C.E.

All in all, sixteen Babylonian horoscopes have been found, ranging from the years 410 B.C.E. to 68 B.C.E., nine Egyptian horoscopes from 37 B.C.E. to 93 C.E., and 180 Greek horoscopes from 61 B.C.E. to about 600 C.E. Considering the fact that hundreds of thousands of nonastrological tablets have been recovered from the earliest down to the latest Babylonian, Egyptian, and Greek periods, this paucity suggests that zodiacal astrology was a new and experimental idea.

With the Babylonian horoscopes, the predictions are scant. Only when one reaches the first and second centuries C.E., as illustrated by Vettius Valens, do predictions become lengthy and involved.

HISTORY FROM ASTROLOGERS

We should mistrust what some astrologers say about the history of astrology. Manly Hall, in *The Story of Astrology*, notes that,

> In his first book on Divination, Cicero observed that the Chaldeans had records of the stars for the space of 370,000 years; and Diodorus Siculus says that their observations comprehended the space of 473,000 years. Thomas Taylor in Notes on Julius Firmicus Maternus says that Epigenes, Berosus, and Critodemes set the duration of astronomical observations by the Babylonians at from 490,000 to 720,000 years. Cicero further maintains that the Babylonians over a period of many thousands of years kept the nativities (horoscopes) of all children who were born among them, and from this enormous mass of data calculated the effects of the various planets and zodiacal signs. What boasted science of the moderns can be said to be built upon a more substantial basis?

Chaldean astrological time-spans have been exaggerated since antiquity. Berossus (ca. 275 B.C.E.) spoke of 468,000 years of compilations, close to the 470,000 mentioned by Cicero. The Greek historian Diodorus (ca. 50 B.C.E.) reported a 473,000 year figure (Diodorus felt that to toy with history was acceptable, feeling that histories are appendages to oratory and need to be adorned with variety). The astrologer Epigenes of Byzantium (ca. 220 B.C.E.) wrote that the Babylonians had tablets comprising 730,000 years of astronomical observations. The astrologer Critodemus (ca. 250 B.C.E.) put the figure at 490,000 years.

The error was obviously perpetuated by Hall. Also, in the Hall book, if we look carefully, we have received the information third- and even fourth-hand: through Hall, Taylor, Cicero, and the Chaldeans.

Hall's account brings us to a clearly impossible situation. The Mesopotamians at this period must have belonged to late *Homo erectus* or early *Homo sapiens,* precursors of modern man. This hominid was slightly over five feet tall with a heavy skull, broad nose, pronounced brow-ridge, sloping forehead, and little chin. The brain size was three-fourths that of modern man, and brain development, lacking frontal lobe evolvement, did not include much language. He possessed the intelligence to manufacture a hand axe and other crude tools of flint and bone as well as to make use of fire enough to cook food, hunt gazelle and boar, and drive rhinoceroses into the bog.

Ruth Hale Oliver, former chairman of the American Federation of Astrologers, suggests that,

> When trying to project the material into the very distant past, I have come to the working conclusion that the zodiac was born during what we call the Cancerian Age; that is, roughly between 8000 and 6000 B.C.E.

At this time, nomadic man had barely settled at Jarmo in 8000 B.C.E. and Jericho in 7000 B.C.E. No celestial notations during this time period have been uncovered.

Joanna Woolfolk, in *The Only Astrology Book You'll Ever Need,* states:

> The study of the Sun, the Moon, stars, eclipses, day and night, began well before recorded history. There are reindeer bones and tusks of mammoths from the Ice Age that have notches carved on them picturing the phases of the Moon. These bones and tusks are dated between 25,000 and 10,000 B.C., and some scientists place them as long ago as 32,000 B.C.!

> . . . The path of the stars was recorded 6000 years before Christ was born. As early as 2767 B.C. a horoscope was cast in Egypt by Imhotep, the architect of the great Step pyramid in Saqqarah. That horoscope still exists!

. . . You can still read star charts that were made by Egyptian astrologers in 4200 B.C.

. . . Hindus trace their religious wisdom back to seven ancient sages known as the Rishis (5000 B.C.).

. . . Some historians mark the beginning of Chinese astrology during the reign of the Divine Emperor Fu Hsi around 2800 B.C.

Notations on rock walls, bones, and stones found scattered between Spain and the Ukraine, dating to about 33,500 B.C.E., have been studied by the science writer Alexander Marshack who feels they are phases of the moon. Most researchers feel that this is a primitive tallying procedure. An example is a bone plaque marked with rows of gouged holes arranged in groups. The first notations of celestial events were pictographs in 3300 B.C.E. Early tablets (ca. 1100 B.C.E.) referred to "stars in the path of the Moon." Imhotep lived about 2670 B.C.E. No horoscope has been found from this time.

Babylonian star lore migrated to Egypt about 600 B.C.E. Although some state the Egyptians had an earlier acquaintance with the stars, no evidence has been found to support the claim. From the Near East, astrology/astronomy made its way to India and the Far East (ca. 450 B.C.E.). Astrological prophecies discovered in China appear to be copies from the library of King Assurbanipal (669–626 B.C.E.).

HOUSES OF THE ZODIAC

How old are the "houses" of the zodiac? That is, when did the supplementary twelve 30-degree arcs based upon the daily rotation of the earth on its axis and commencing with the sign rising at birth and denoting love, death, marriage, self, and so forth, begin to appear in the horoscope? Most astrological historians assign this innovation to the Arab Al-Battan, or Albategnius (850–929 C.E.). In fact, this was a Greek addition described in the *Tetrabiblos* and utilized in Greek horoscopes as "loci" superimposed on zodiacal signs.

OTHER CIVILIZATIONS

Similarities exist between the ziggurats of the Mesopotamians, the pyramids of the Egyptians, and the ancient sun-temples of the Incas, Aztecs, and Mayans. The implication is that these civilizations may have been, at some time, a part of an earlier one, now extinct. This viewpoint is rejected for two reasons.

The first is the fact that the earliest American temple was built by the Aztecs in Oaxaca about 500 B.C.E., and the first real sun-temple at Teotihuacan was not constructed until 100 C.E. The first pyramid was built in Egypt about 2900 B.C.E., and the earliest ziggurat was constructed about 3000 B.C.E. It is possible that nomadic Egyptians and Mesopotamians exchanged ideas, then migrated to the Americas and influenced the art of temple construction, but this is unlikely.

A more compelling reason is the fact that these structures were built for different reasons. In the case of the Sumerians, it was to facilitate the descent, in some form, of the gods to earth, and to note movements of wandering stars and report omens.

With the Egyptians, it was so the soul of the mummified body could have quick and easy access to the heavens. In predynastic Egypt, the dead were buried on the edge of the desert in shallow graves over which were piled rectangular mounds of sand. From that time on the mound merely increased in size. The pyramidal structure represented the rays of the sun by which the king could transport himself at will to and from the sun god Ra. The purpose was to preserve the king's mummified body for eternity.

In early American civilizations, the temple was built to commune with the sun. The Aztecs, Incas, and Mayans worshiped the sun, although moon worship entered in at various times. The Aztecs, and their predecessors the Toltecs, felt that the sun brought life by his daily appearance. Atop the pyramid was the temple, or temples. Tenochtitlan had two temples. One was for the national god, the Hummingbird Wizard, who was the sun, and the other was for the rain god.

No trace of an older pyramid-type structure other than Egyptian or Mesopotamian has been found anywhere in the world, including undersea excavation.

SUMMARY

In a loose historical sense, astrological prediction began in the second millennium, zodiacal astrology was created in the fifth century B.C.E., and horoscopic astrology reached a refined form about 200 C.E. with Ptolemy and Vettius Valens. Other horoscopes were undoubtedly made during this time, but not much earlier, since the zodiac was not invented until 418 B.C.E., and the mathematics necessary to derive the 30-degree zodiacal signs was itself derived only a few years earlier. Each step was dependent upon the other. Talk of horoscopes, or even of the zodiac, as existing much before the fifth century B.C.E. must be dismissed as nonsense.

8

Do the Sun, Moon, Planets, and Stars Affect Life on Earth?

R. S. Richardson, of the Griffith Observatory in Los Angeles, wrote in *The Fascinating World of Astronomy* that the sun is the only body outside the earth itself that is really necessary for our existence. People often suppose that the gravitational attraction of the stars and planets keeps the universe in a delicate state of balance, so that the slightest upset of the forces involved would lead to disaster. As a matter of fact, all the bodies in the universe could be destroyed except the sun, earth, and possibly the moon, and few people would ever be aware of the fact.

THE SUN AND THE MOON

Astrologers often use (seize on, perhaps) studies of the sun, moon, and planets to validate astrology. Does the sun affect life on earth? The answer is yes. When the sun goes down, some biological organisms (excluding nocturnal species) sleep. The twenty-four-hour sun-cycle is involved with many species, including man. In prolonged light or darkness, the brain creates a substitute, or *circadian* (circa:

approximate; dian: day) day. In addition, the movement of earth around the sun each year causes the seasons, which affect man in obvious ways.

Ocean tides are caused by the gravitational pull of the sun and moon. Because of the rotation of the earth on its axis, two tides are present each day. One high tide occurs when we face the moon, and a second when we are directly opposite. In addition, monthly and yearly tides exist.

Tides affect spawning and food availability (shore dwellers follow the ebb and flow of tides). Many species show daily, monthly, and yearly cycles in relation to tides. In Bermuda, shrimp swarm before midnight of the new moon once a year. Once a year, at high tide, grunion swarm onto the lower beaches of California. The marine worm, pololo, comes up from the sea floor near Samoa and Fiji to spawn during the last quarter of the November moon, and is eaten by the natives. The opening of oyster shells, the sex lives of rats, the metabolic fluctuations of fiddler crabs, snails, salamanders, earthworms, smelt, as well as potatoes, carrots, and seaweed are involved with tides and cycles.

Sunspots are cyclonic storms of gaseous matter that stream out from the sun and create electromagnetic fields. In 1930, H. T. Stetson of the Massachusetts Institute of Technology found a correlation between sunspot maximum and stock-market fluctuations, vintage years for wines, and tree-ring growth. Stetson suggested that increased solar radiation seemed to "push men, directly or indirectly, into things." Later studies showed no correlation.

A Tallahassee ear, nose and throat surgeon, E. J. Andrews, logged a thousand tonsillectomy cases from 1956 through 1958 and observed that the majority of "bleeders" occurred between the first quarter and full moon. He then did a similar study on bleeding ulcers, with a similar result. Bleeding studies have since been repeated showing only chance results.

In 1960, a psychiatrist at the University of Pennsylvania, L. J. Ravitz, measured changes in electrical potential in normal versus psychotic patients and found electrical potential increases around the new and full moons, as well as seasonal variations. Acutely disturbed persons showed the highest voltage increase. These studies have not been repeated or substantiated.

Many, including some of my medical colleagues, have suggested that the full moon favors crime, hospitalizations, and an increase in birth rate. Abell and Greenspan studied births at UCLA and found no correlation between numbers of births and the full moon, or any other phase of the moon. Pokorny and others have shown no pattern to suicides, homicides, or admissions to mental hospitals.

Some feel that intrinsic cycles (biorhythms) are present in man. A twenty-three-day "physical" cycle, a twenty-eight-day "sensitivity" cycle, and a thirty-three-day "intellectual" cycle are said to exist. Hines found no evidence to support the claims.

THE PLANETS

Do the planets affect life on earth from any known energy source: electromagnetic, geomagnetic, radiational, or gravitational? Bok said that the gravitational forces at birth produced by the doctor and nurse and by the furniture in the delivery room outweigh celestial forces.

The planet Venus, home of the goddess of love, is covered by yellow, sulfuric-acid-covered clouds of carbon dioxide and is extremely hot (the mean surface temperature is 867° F). On the other hand, Mars, considered fiery by the ancients because of its reddish glow, is below freezing (the mean temperature is –72° F; the redness is caused by reflected light from iron-oxide-containing dust, suspended smoglike in the Martian atmosphere). With the exception of Mercury, which is closest to the sun, all of the other planets, including Jupiter, are below freezing. Culver observed that the moon, Venus, and Mars have no magnetic fields at all.

However, two astrologically oriented scientists—Percy Seymour, an astronomer, and Frank McGillion, a pharmacologist—suggest that the sun, moon, and planets are in geomagnetic vibrational synchrony (resonance) with humans. Resonant interactions affect the nervous system and thus the personality (Dean—as well as Seymour—notes that planetary forces are below the lower limit for a biological response. Seymour's theory is that resonance deals with only a small amount of energy). McGillion believes that the pineal gland is involved. (See chapter 9.)

The horoscope also involves apparent positions and not actual positions of the planets. For example, the four-hour light-time from Neptune puts it roughly sixty degrees ahead of where it seems to be.

J. H. Nelson, a radio weatherman for RCA, found that severe radio disturbances seemed to be associated with certain planetary angular configurations. Magnetic storms, more evident with increased sunspot activity, seemed to be present during periods of 0, 90, 180, and 270 degree planetary configurations (adverse astrological aspects).

Nelson's data were investigated by Geoffrey Dean, a technical editor in Australia. After a reexamination of eighteen years of Nelson's daily forecasts, no evidence was found to support the claim that planetary positions correlate with shortwave radio quality. The planets performed no better than chance.

A sidelight concerning Nelson's data is that it is based on a heliocentric system, not the geocentric one used in horoscopes. The "aspects" formed between planets in a heliocentric system are not those formed in a geocentric one, because we are now on the sun, standing and looking out, and not on the earth. (If we on earth looked out and saw Jupiter in 4 degrees of the sign of Aries and Saturn at 4 degrees of Capricorn—then if we traveled instantaneously to the sun 93 million miles away—we would see these planets against another backdrop of degrees and signs.) The Nelson data was thus also in error astrologically.

A unique study was done in 1959 by Rudolf Tomaschek, a geophysics professor at the University of Munich, who studied 134 major earthquakes and found that in all cases the planet Uranus was directly overhead at the exact moment of the quake. Since that time, studies have been repeated, with chance results.

Mars has generated one of the more turbulent controversies in astrology. In the late 1960s, 1970s, and into the 1980s, a French psychologist, Michel Gauquelin, analyzed the horoscopes of several thousand European sports people. He found that in the birth horoscopes of sports champions the rising (rising sign) or culminating (midheaven) of the planet Mars was above chance expectations. The studies were repeated over the years, in Europe and the United States, with equivocal results. The study became known as the "Mars Effect."

Further studies, including those by the Committee for the Scientific Investigation of Claims of the Paranormal (CSICOP) in the United States, as well as a similar French committee, concluded after painstaking research there was no evidence for the "Mars Effect." Multiple analyses of sports champions from various countries indicated that Mars rising or culminating was at chance.

The "Mars Effect," however, has not died out, and in astrological circles has spawned the notion that if enough studies are done over a long enough period of time, a correlation will be found between planets and professions (or something similar) in some way. This school of thought suggests that the Babylonians must have followed some kind of scientific method in order to derive the results that Ptolemy and others compiled. This is the essence of today's astrology: "Keep looking at planetary configurations until you find something."

THE STARS

Astrology contends that the sun, moon, and planets are "in" a particular sign, or in earlier times constellation, of the zodiac. This is inaccurate. These bodies are seen against a background of nonrelated stars that have been artificially grouped into a constellation. Stars have no connection with one another, nor do constellations, nor do galaxies. They are tens, hundreds, thousands, and millions of light-years away from one another and from the earth. Some stars in a constellation may be close, others very far away—even outside of our galaxy. In fact, several galaxies are seen in many zodiacal constellations.

How do the stars affect us? No gravitational force acts at those distances and the power, in terms of radiation falling on earth from the most intense radio sources, is about 100 watts of which only .00000000000001 watts are intercepted by a giant radio telescope. The electromagnetic force-field of the earth is unchanged by this.

9

Birth versus Conception, and Twins

The horoscope is derived from the degree of the arc of the sign of the zodiac on the horizon (ascendant) at the moment and place of birth. Most astrologers use the time of birth to create the horoscope, but some use the time of conception (the majority of astrologers consider the time of conception too uncertain). Interestingly, Ptolemy prefers conception time over birth time, a hoary thorn in things:

> The chronological starting-point of human nativities is naturally the very time of conception, but potentially and accidentally the moment of birth, in cases in which the very time of conception is known either by chance or by observation, it is more fitting that we should follow it in determining the special nature of body and soul, examining the effective power of the configuration of the stars at that time.

Conception can never be known within less than a five-day period, a fact not appreciated in Ptolemy's time. The egg lives for seventy-two hours and sperm survive in the female genital tract for two days. Fertilization depends upon when ovulation occurs, which may be any time during the life of the spermatozoon, or predating it by seventy-two hours (or, forty-eight hours plus seventy-two hours equals 120 hours. This implies that only one coitus had occurred during this period. If more than one occurred the time would be further extended).

Carl Jung maintained that "whatever is born or done this moment of time, has the qualities of this moment of time." J. Tucker, former editor of *Science and Astrology* magazine, refined this line of thinking:

> In the moments prior to birth the child has no separate existence but consists of a collection of living cells which may well be considered part of the mother's organism. But, at the moment of drawing its first breath, a vital change takes place. For it is at that critical moment that self-animation comes to the child—the product of the life-forces which enter it. And, at that same moment, the lines of force of the existing magnetic field surrounding the Earth (product or resultant of the composite magnetic fields belonging to the Sun, Moon, Planets and Stars) run through the child's body, setting the paths of the electrons within the atoms of the matter composing the child's body into a fixed and definite pattern which appears to exist for the duration of its life.

The astronomer Percy Seymour, an advocate for astrology, furthered this line of thinking in 1988 with the suggestion that the fetus responds to geomagnetic fluctuations of the sun, moon, and planets (resonance). The fetus picks up subtle resonant "music" via the nervous system. This Seymour designates as "magnetic memories" or "genetic tuning."

The magnetic field of the earth, if it does have a moment-to-moment effect upon biology, which is unlikely, must also affect the developing embryo and fetus. Since birth may be thought of, in the mammalian sense, as a stage in the maturation of the organism, and since the baby is very much alive and kicking before expulsion from the uterus, one could ask, when might "electron fixation" or "resonance fixation" occur along the gestational route? At conception?

At potential viability, which is mid-pregnancy? At viability, which is thirty-six weeks? The answer is that they do not occur.

TWINS

Once per month a female of child-bearing age expels an egg from an ovary into the abdominal cavity (ovulation). The egg enters the Fallopian tube and moves to the uterus. After coitus, sperm travel into the cervix, uterus and up both tubes. Fertilization occurs when one spermatozoon enters the egg. The fertilized egg divides and moves down the tube to the uterus where it implants and matures into an embryo and fetus.

Occasionally a fertilized egg cleaves into two, three, or more units in the tube and each unit develops into an embryo. These are identical twins (or triplets, etc.) and are always of the same sex. All of the chromosomes containing all of the genes are duplicated.

Sometimes two eggs are expelled during ovulation and both are fertilized. Each implants and develops into a separate embryo. These are nonidentical or fraternal twins and may be of either sex, the same as any brother or sister. The genes are different, since they come from a different egg and spermatozoon.

Since astrology maintains that individuals born at the same time will have similar destinies because all celestial formations and magnetic force fields are the same, identical twins pose no problem. It can be shown that most do, in fact, have similar life patterns, as evidenced by thousands of multiple-birth case studies. The problem arises with nonidentical twins. They are usually not in the least similar. Or, they are as similar as any two siblings might be. They do not lead the same kinds of lives and do not have similar life patterns or goals. It is because they are different genetically.

10

Sign versus Constellation, and the Aquarian Age

Today, signs of the zodiac differ from constellations because of the precession (the moving back) of the equinoxes. Because the earth wobbles slightly on its axis much as does a top—one degree backward every 71.1 years—the constellations no longer coincide with the seasons in which they were noted in Ptolemy's time (150 C.E.). The constellations have shifted forward about 30 degrees—one complete sign (more correctly, the earth has shifted backward). In the days of Hipparchus and Ptolemy, the sun was at 9 degrees in the constellation of Aries at the vernal equinox, March 21. Today on March 21 the sun is 9 degrees in the constellation of Pisces. Thus, constellationally speaking, those individuals born, for example, between March 21 and April 20 should no longer be Arians but Pisceans, and so on back around the zodiac (see figure 43).

Since we cannot see the sign or constellation that the sun is in at a particular month because of the brightness of the sun, the question arises as to whether the ancients used, as the monthly sign, the constellation preceding the rising of the sun in the east. If so, then we are really two signs back instead of one.

Astrologers have two thoughts on this. *Constellation,* or *sidereal,*

	Sign	Constellation
Aries	March 21	April 18
Taurus	April 20	May 14
Gemini	May 21	June 21
Cancer	June 21	July 20
Leo	July 23	August 10
Virgo	August 23	September 16
Libra	September 23	October 31
Scorpio	October 23	November 23
Sagittarius	November 22	December 17
Capricorn	December 22	January 19
Aquarius	January 20	February 16
Pisces	February 19	March 11

Fig. 43: Dates of sun entering signs and constellations. From *Information Please Almanac,* Simon and Schuster, 1976.

astrologers, rare in the Western world, maintain that the *constellations* through which the sun and planets travel during the year is the essential point, even though today they differ from the signs, and follow the precession. The sidereal argument is that ancient principles are based upon unique powers of the constellations and cannot be ignored even if the constellations are in different signs. Sidereal astrology is practiced mainly in Eastern countries such as India, and is usually accompanied by concepts involving karma.

Tropical, or *sign,* astrologers (modern Western astrology) follow the signs and ignore the precession. They counter by indicating that the ancients based sign interpretation on the seasons, then named the constellations. To reclassify an Aquarian, for instance, as a flinty wintry Capricorn just because during the centuries the constellation of Capricorn has moved forward to February (actually the earth moved backward) is unthinkable.

Sign astrologers also submit that "lingering effects" exist from the "original" constellations. It seems inconceivable, however, that the effects of the "original" constellation of Aries, for example, would linger around all twelve signs of the zodiac. Then there is the question of what is the "original" sign? Today the vernal equinox is in the constellation of Pisces. In Ptolemy's time (150 C.E.) it was in Aries, in ancient Mesopotamia (ca. 2000 B.C.E.) in Taurus, before that (ca. 4000 B.C.E.) in Gemini, and so on. With this logic, there are no original signs. Either all signs are the original ones or no signs are. So we are either all signs of the zodiac or none.

Seasons are a stumbling block to traditional, or sign astrology, since they differ according to latitude. Those described in Mesopotamian literature lie within a belt of 6 degrees in the northern hemisphere. South of the equator they are reversed. In Australia, South America and South Africa, for example, the sunny season is December, January, and February, and the winter months are June, July, and August. Near the South Pole continuous light is present during our fall and winter. Thus a seasonal system becomes virtually meaningless.

In the year 2607 the last degree of the constellation of Aquarius will contain the sun on March 21, heralding, evidently, the long-awaited "Aquarian Age," although some astrologers feel the Aquarian Age is upon us, having begun in 1904 (an inaccuracy of seven centuries). Why the constellation containing the sun at the vernal equinox connotes an "age" is a mystery.

However, if we are to believe traditional astrology, we must not recognize the change in constellation at the vernal equinox, since constellations are discounted. Therefore, different ages cannot exist, since they all depend upon the constellation the sun is in on March 21.

11

Selective Memory, or the Versatile Human Mind

One of the interesting aspects of astrology is how adaptable (some would say slightly unstable), or versatile, is the human mind. For most of us, we are what we are told we are.

For example, most people born between August 22 and September 21 think of themselves as Virgos. A person in this group may say that all of the astrology stuff is nonsense, but he still thinks of himself as a Virgo. He may not believe in casting horoscopes and all that, but every once in a while he reads about Virgo in the horoscope section of the newspaper. He thinks, I wonder if there is anything to this? He does not realize, at that point, that he is already hooked. He is a believer.

THE APPEAL OF ASTROLOGY

The astrology section of the *Encyclopedia of the Paranormal* summarizes the appeal of astrology in the following way: sun signs are popular because they fill a need, they are simple, and they seem to work. "Seem to work" should be more properly redefined as "are satisfying." The reasons for this include:

128

You have a great need for other people to like you and admire you. You have a tendency to be critical of yourself. You have a great deal of unused capacity which you have not used to your advantage. While you have some personality weaknesses, you are generally able to compensate for them. Your sexual adjustment has presented problems for you. Disciplined and self-controlled outside, you tend to be worrisome and insecure inside. At times you have serious doubts as to whether you have made the right decision or done the right thing. You prefer a certain amount of change and variety and become dissatisfied when hemmed in by restrictions and limitations. You pride yourself on being an independent thinker and do not accept others' statements without satisfactory proof. You have found it unwise to be too frank in revealing yourself to others. At times you are extroverted, affable, and sociable, while at other times you are introverted, wary, and reserved. Some of your aspirations tend to be pretty unrealistic. Security is one of your major goals in life.

Fig. 44: P. T. Barnum Effect. From Christopher French et al., "Belief in Astrology: A Test of the Barnum Effect." *Skeptical Inquirer* 15 (Winter 1991): 166–72.

1. A search for personal identity.
2. A religious belief system.
3. Simplicity.
4. Talking about ourselves.
5. Perceived validity.
6. Availability.

Let us examine, for a moment, some of the ways the mind works, such as the *P. T. Barnum effect* and *selective memory*, or selective thinking, important tools of astrology.

THE P. T. BARNUM EFFECT

Named after the famous circus entrepreneur, the *Barnum* concept involves two ideas: (1) have a little something for everyone, and (2) there's a sucker born every minute. Elaborate studies, using refined statistical methods, have shown that this effect is an important ingredient not only in astrology but also in psychic readings, palmistry, the reading of Tarot cards, selling automobiles, and politics.

Figure 44 is a typical Barnum profile. If told that it belonged to his sun sign, someone reading the above might be impressed by its accuracy. This does not mean that astrologers are dishonest. It means that astrology has evolved into a Barnum framework so as to make prediction feasible.

The concept was not lost on ancient Mesopotamian priests when reporting omens of one sort or another. They became quite good at it, and were able to report on celestial phenomena and on the shapes of animal intestines and livers with a positive slant. If the reporting required negativity, a nebulous drift was divined interspersed with occasional positive messages.

Figure 45 shows a rather average random omen report of the early first millennium B.C.E. Although at first glance it seems straightforward, let's look at it carefully. "When the moon occults (eclipses) Jupiter, a king will die that year." A great many kings ruled in 1000 B.C.E., and every year some of them died.

"When Jupiter enters the midst of the Moon, there will be want in Aharru." Want is universal. "The king of Elam will be slain with the sword. . . ." The most common way to be slain, including kings, was with the sword. Again, no time frame is given for the slaying. If it does not take place soon, the implication is that it is destined for the future. "When Jupiter enters the midst of the Moon, the market of the land will be low." The marketplace is always low to most citizens. "When Jupiter goes out from behind the Moon, there will be hostility in the land." Another safe occurrence, somewhere in the land. The scribe, or priest, Asharidu concludes with two obsequious positives and indicates he is the king's servant.

If you were the king to whom Asharidu wrote his clay message, you might be impressed.

When the Moon occults Jupiter, that year a king will die, (or) an eclipse of the Moon and Sun will take place. A great king will die. When Jupiter enters the midst of the Moon, there will be want in Aharru. The King of Elam will be slain with the sword: in Subarti ———— (?) will revolt. When Jupiter enters the midst of the Moon, the market of the land will be low. When Jupiter goes out from behind the Moon, there will be hostility in the land.

After two hours of the night had passed, a great star shone from north to south. Its omens are propitious for the king's desire. The King of Akkad will accomplish his mission.

From Asharidu (the greater), the king's servant.

Fig. 45: Omen report (ca. 1000 B.C.E). From R. C. Thompson, *The Reports of the Magicians and Astrologers of Nineveh and Babylon,* Luzac and Company, 1900.

SELECTIVE MEMORY

Selective thinking, or, "if you want to believe it, you will," was illustrated a few years ago by the psychologist Michel Gauquelin early in his career, and again artfully by the magician Randi when he interviewed a biorhythm expert on a radio talk show.

Gauquelin gave 150 people a ten-page computer interpretation supposedly of their own birth chart but which was actually that of a notorious mass murderer. Ninety percent found the accuracy confirmed by family and friends. Ninety-four percent found it accurately described their characters, personal problems, and cycles of events in their lives.

On his radio show, Randi requested a biorhythm chart for himself and his secretary, and selected a listener who agreed to accept a free chart in return for a report at the end of two months stating how successful the chart was. The listener promised to keep a day-by-day diary and to rate the chart for accuracy.

At the end of two months, the listener phoned and told Randi that he should take this matter very seriously, that her chart was "at least 90 percent accurate." In reality, purposely, she had been sent Randi's own chart. He blamed the error on his secretary. He then sent her his secretary's chart, which he said was the correct one. She was thrilled and reported that this one was "even more accurate." He then told her she had received his secretary's chart. "There was a short pause, then a snort, and the woman hung up," related Randi.

In other words, it is possible to trick people into the realization of a delusion. It may not seem fair, but the depth of the delusion may require drastic measures to illuminate the fallacy.

Another case of the adaptability of the mind is the believer on the border (cusp) of two signs. He must perform mental gymnastics to keep pace with both, which he often does with alacrity. Or consider the believer who has been incorrectly told his birthday. Perhaps he was adopted as a child. After many years, he learns his correct birthday. What will happen? Answer: he will shed the ways of the old sign and adopt those of the new. He will say he was never "comfortable" with his old sign. He will open the new horoscope and point out that if you look carefully at the progression of Saturn in the twelfth house . . .

In my experience, the closest to the above was a friend who had himself in the wrong sign, living for many years as a Scorpio. He would comment from time to time how appropriate the sign of Scorpio was for him, with its intensity and power. One day by chance he told me his birthday. I laughed and told him he was not a Scorpio but a Sagittarius. He was silent. "Really?" I could hear wheels working. Since he knew I was writing an "astrology book," I took advantage of the occasion and offered to draw up a horoscope. Sure enough, he was a Sagittarian: three planets in Sagittarius, only the sun in Scorpio. I took the opportunity to present a brief critique of astrology. "Interesting," he replied.

I observed him over the next few months. He never discussed astrology again, but his wife told me he occasionally scans the horoscope section in the newspaper. "Which sign does he look at?" I inquired. "Both of them," she replied. If he does not give up the entire thing, I have no doubt he will gradually adapt to his new sign.

12

Questions

How could an astronomer of Ptolemy's stature write a book on astrology?

Ptolemy's stature has been, and is, questioned—particularly regarding manipulation of data in the *Almagest*. His motives for compiling astrological data are unknown, other than perhaps, along with his works in astronomy, music, and geography, creating a reputation as a renowned Alexandrian scholar.

From fragments of writings in Ptolemy's time and somewhat later, he comes across as stuffy, perhaps a bit of a snob. To some he is eclectic; to others syncretic. He refers to one philosopher by name, Aristotle, and then only in passing. He mentions none of his famous Alexandrian predecessors except Hipparchus. Jones notes that Ptolemy dismisses those who followed Hipparchus with contemptuous allusions or disdainful silence.

The translator of the *Tetrabiblos*, F. E. Robbins, indicates that the earliest Greek text of the *Tetrabiblos* is only of the thirteenth century. The text has been printed three times, in 1535, 1553, and 1581. Translations of the *Tetrabiblos* have been more numerous than texts. The oldest is the Arabic version, made in the ninth century. There are in European libraries at least thirty-five manuscripts containing all, or a large part, of the *Tetrabiblos*. While some have questioned the authenticity of the authorship of the *Tetrabiblos*, Robbins believes Ptolemy wrote it, since the language and astronomy follow that of his other works (i.e., the *Almagest*). However, it should be noted that some scholars question the authenticity of the *Tetrabiblos*.

The *Almagest* was the standard text in astronomy for a thousand years. The Arabs referred to it as "The Greatest." The writer Hephaestion of Thebes, in 381, called Ptolemy "The Divine Ptolemy." From all of the available evidence accumulated so far, we would characterize Ptolemy as "The Great Compiler," and note that a number of his compilations have been shown to be in error.

Some feel a possible tie may have existed to the Roman emperor Hadrian (76–138) who reigned during Ptolemy's time (100–178) and was the only astrologer-emperor. Hadrian or his adopted successor, Antoninus Pius (138–161), would likely have had to approve Ptolemy's appointment to the Museum at Alexandria.

What is the importance of prediction in astrology?

Prediction is the essence of astrology. Priests in Sumer who were able to predict successfully were richly rewarded. Early predictions consisted of correlating weather activity and celestial phenomena such as phases of the moon and eclipses with the future of the king and the city-state. Later, internal organs of sheep were examined and predictions were made on that basis. Priests who were successful at prediction enjoyed an enviable reputation.

Incorrect predictions often resulted in banishment or death. Consequently, priests began to accumulate knowledge with more sophistication. The sun, moon, stars, and planets usually moved in a predictable way. If cycles could be computed, predictions could be made with safety. This is an important reason for the birth of ancient astronomy and mathematics—the potential for successful prediction. The birth horoscope is the ultimate predictive document, gone awry.

What are the origins of the signs of the zodiac? What are the sun signs? What makes me a Leo?

This question is critical for advocates of astrology. The sun signs are the "signs" of the zodiac through which the sun passes each month. When someone asks, "What is your sign?" they mean sun sign. Signs were named after constellations. Constellations were named in a superficial, rather offhanded fashion by the Sumerians and Akkadians. Many constellations (including the twelve zodiacal ones) described in mul.APIN date back to about 1000 B.C.E., but most were older than Assyrian. The Mesopotamians were striving for a calendar and used the fixed stars (constellations) as reference points for seasons, since particular stars always appeared at the same time each year.

A Sumerian priest was likely talking to two farmers one night. "I am designing a calendar," he said. "I want to name the star clusters through which the gods pass each season so that we can have reference points. I need names for points of reference." He paused and picked up the reed stylus. "Let's start with midsummer." "Name them scorpion," said Sin-Samuh. "One stung my foot last year at this time." "It was later," said Zakir. "He bit you in the fall." Sin-Samuh thought. "Maybe it was later." "We may use that name, then, for later," said the priest. "What about a lion?" asked Zakir. "One big guy chased Ben's wife the other day, but I think he was looking for water. The creek is dry." "Lion, huh?" The priest thought for a moment. "Not bad." They looked at the quiet, starry night sky. "I see a paw." "I see the body, over there." "No, that's the mane." Sin-Samuh moved his hand in the air. "See how it curves down." "I think you're right, Sam," said the priest. He pressed the stylus into the wet clay. "Then lion it will be."

This is the reason you are a Leo, I a Scorpio. Nothing more.

Where did the symbols for the planets and signs of the zodiac come from?

Symbols were absent in the original documents, both tablets and papyri. They began appearing in Byzantine manuscripts of the tenth century C.E.

Ancient astrology/astronomy is often depicted as inseparable. Did many of the ancient astronomers not *believe in astrology?*

From fairly early on some scientists, philosophers, and others rejected the idea of divination. Cicero mentions that the Greek astronomer and mathematician Eudoxus (400–347 B.C.E.) indicated, "One must least of all believe the Chaldeans with regard to their detailed prediction of a person's life on the basis of the day of his birth." Ennius (239–169 B.C.E.), a Roman poet, criticized the stargazer:

> He observes the signs of the astrologi what happens in the sky, when the goat or the scorpion or the name of some other animal of Jove rises. Not one of them pays attention to what lies before his feet. Raptly they gaze at the realms of heaven.

The Greek philosopher Carneades (214–129 B.C.E.) opposed astrology. Cicero (106–43 B.C.E.) was an example of someone who reflected about astrology in his early years, but later in life in his essays *On Fate* and *On Divination* rejected it. Lucretius (94–55 B.C.E.), Roman philosopher and poet, wrote a long poem in six books, *On the Nature of Things,* which criticizes fatalism and astrology. Epictetus (55–135 C.E.), a Greek slave who became a Stoic philosopher, and who taught in Rome and later in Greece during the latter part of Ptolemy's time, wrote:

> For what can the diviner see, besides death, or danger, or in short things of this kind? When it is necessary to expose oneself to danger for a friend, or even a duty to die for him, what occasion have I for divination? Have I not a diviner within, who has told me the essence of good and evil . . . ? What further need, then, have I of the entrails of victims, or the flight of birds? . . .

> What, then, is it that leads us so often to divination? Cowardice, the dread of events. Hence we flatter the diviners: "Pray, sir, shall I inherit my father's estate?" "Let us see, let me sacrifice upon the occasion." "Nay, sir, just as Fortune pleases." Then, if he says, "You

shall inherit it," we give him thanks, as if we received the inheritance from him. The consequence is that they play on us.

The famous Neoplatonist philosopher Plotinus (205–270 C.E.) mentions the stars and planets in his treatise, the *Second Ennead*:

> More absurdly still, some of them are supposed to be malicious and others to be helpful, and yet the evil stars will bestow favors and the benevolent act harshly: further, their action alters as they see each other or not, so that, after all, they possess no definite nature but vary according to their angles of aspect; a star is kindly when it sees one of its fellows but changes at sight of another.

Why do people believe in astrology?

It is a unique and magical way of looking at life.

Conclusion

Today astrology has moved into an elusive position. Ronald Davison, former president of the astrological lodge of the Theosophic Society in London, explained: "Astrology deals not only with the nature of things but with their latent possibilities, which are located in a dimension not apparent to our five senses." Manly Hall says: "The stimuli of planetary groupings operating through the magnetic fields of the earth cause definite and measurable effects, and these effects are sympathetically communicated to all creatures functioning within themselves polarizations of universal principles."

One cannot argue with the first statement, except to point out other words which could be substituted for "astrology," such as, perhaps, God, ESP, or telepathy. The second hypothesis is equally nebulous, besides being factually incorrect. Other innovative efforts at explanations or clarifications are comparably dismal. Carroll Righter indicates that the stars "impel," they do not "compel." Ruth Oliver sees the horoscope as a "diagram of potentialities"—two murky comments.

Many accept the abundance of paleontologic evidence showing the origins of astrology, as well as to many of the criticisms posed in this book. A common condescension is that genes do dictate behavioral characteristics—but so does the time of birth, in a general "potential" way. So one must look to the horoscope for a complete evaluation. "Universal polarities" exist, governed by cycles, probably in a monthly way, and usually relating in some fashion to the solar year. A keen eye, however, will recognize these modifications and defenses as an attempt to bypass past errors.

Some use the works of Ravitz, Andrews, Tomaschek, Nelson, and others to point out the close association between celestial rhythms and astrology. To me it has the opposite effect. It shows that conditions and catastrophes happen to all people, not just to a select few.

As mentioned in chapter 8, after the "Mars Effect," today's astrologers have suggested to keep looking at planetary configurations until something is found. This seems to be a last-ditch effort to salvage credibility.

A voice may now be nipping at the souls of believers. It goes something like this: "I was born on April 4. I am an Aries. I *feel* like an Aries. I've read all the signs and the only one that makes any sense for me is Aries. Regardless of what you say, I *know* I'm an Aries."

We have sort of tested this little hypothesis. A compendium of the twelve signs from seven leading astrology works was compiled. The test was designed only for those who had three or more planets in the sun sign, had two or less in any other sign, and were more than eight degrees from a cusp. Nine astrologers verified that the compendium offered a fair representation of the signs. The test must be done on persons who know nothing of the signs, an *extremely* difficult problem. We found that of thirty-seven persons tested, thirty-six picked the incorrect sun sign as more accurately representing them than any other. They were given a second choice. Two picked the correct sign.

Because of the prodigious amount of proastrology material available, a more rigorous critical look at astrology is vital, including (1) an accurate early history with whys and whos (this book), (2) ongoing statistical evidence showing the randomness of horoscopic prediction and interpretation, and (3) the use of innovative ideas to challenge the lore.

Many reject the idea of having to "prove" astrology. "Astrology is the language of individuality and uniqueness," says Caroline Casey. "Statistics by their very nature are about nonindividuality and nonuniqueness. So what if astrology doesn't stand up to scientific testing? What about music? What about poetry? What about religion? Do you want to put music and poetry to a double-blind test?" The answer for music and poetry is no. The answer for astrology is yes.

Bibliography

Abell, G., and B. Greenspan. "The Moon and the Maternity Ward." *Skeptical Inquirer* 3 (Summer 1979): 17–25.

Andrews, E. J. "The Cyclic Periodicity of Postoperative Hemorrhage." *Journal of the Florida Medical Association* 46 (1960): 1362–66.

Aschoff, Juergen, ed. *Circadian Clocks*. Amsterdam: North-Holland Publishing Company, 1985.

Asimov, I. *Words from the Myths*. Boston: Houghton Mifflin Company, 1961.

———. *The Greeks: A Great Adventure*. Boston: Houghton Mifflin Company, 1965.

———. *The Near East: Ten Thousand Years of History*. Boston: Houghton Mifflin Company, 1968.

———. *Asimov's Biographical Encyclopedia of Science and Technology*. Garden City: Doubleday & Co., 1972.

———. *Asimov's Chronology of the World*. New York: HarperCollins, 1991.

"Astrology." In *Encyclopaedia Britannica*. Chicago: William Benton, Pub., 1973.

Baigent, M. *From the Omens of Babylon: Astrology and Ancient Mesopotamia*. London: Penguin/Arkana, 1994.

Bartky, Walter. *Highlights of Astronomy*. Chicago: University of Chicago Press, 1964.

Bastedo, R. "An Empirical Test of Popular Astrology." *Skeptical Inquirer* 3 (Fall 1978): 17–38.

Benski, C., et al. *The "Mars Effect."* Amherst, N.Y.: Prometheus Books, 1996.

Biggs, R. "The Babylonian Prophecies and the Astrological Texts." *Journal of Cuneiform Studies* 37 (1985): 86–90.

Bok, B. "Scientists Look at Astrology: Summary of Report of Committee." *Scientific Monthly* 52 (1941): 233–44.

———. "A Critical Look at Astrology." *Humanist* 35 (1975): 6–9.

Boll, F., and C. Bezold. *Sternglaube und Sterndeutung.* Leipzig: B. G. Teubner, 1918.

Bouchard, T. *Twins as a Tool of Behavioral Genetics: Report of the Dahlem Workshop.* New York: J. Wiley, 1992.

Bouche-Leclercq, A. *L'Astrologie Greque.* Paris: E. Leroux, 1899.

British Museum, Trustees. *A Guide to the Babylonian and Assyrian Antiquities.* London, 1908.

Brown, F. "A Unified Theory for Biological Rhythms." In *Circadian Clocks,* edited by J. Aschoff. Amsterdam: North-Holland Publishing Company, 1965.

Burenhult, G. *The First Humans.* New York: HarperCollins, 1993.

Carlson, Shawn. "A Double-Blind Test of Astrology." *Nature* 318 (December 5, 1985): 419–25.

Carpenter, R., et al. *Everyday Life in Ancient Times.* Washington, D.C.: National Geographic Society, 1961.

Chiera, E. *Sumerian Lexical Texts from the Temple School of Nippur,* vol. 11. Chicago: University of Chicago Oriental Institute Publishers, 1929.

Claridge, G. *Personality Differences and Biological Variations: A Study of Twins.* New York: Pergamon Press, 1973.

Clason, C. B. *Exploring the Distant Stars.* New York: G. P. Putnam's Sons, 1958.

Clay, A., ed. *Babylonian Records.* New Haven, Conn.: Yale University Press, 1923.

Cornell, J. *The First Stargazers.* New York: Charles Scribner's, 1981.

Cramer, F. H. *Astrology in Roman Law and Politics.* Philadelphia: American Philosophical Society, 1954.

Croswell, K. "A Milestone in Fornax." *Astronomy* 23 (1995): 42–47.

Culver, R., and Philip Ianna. *Astrology: True or False?* Amherst, N.Y.: Prometheus Books, 1988.

Cumont, Franz. *The Oriental Religions in Roman Paganism.* London: G. Routledge & Sons, 1911.

Cumont, Franz. *Astrology and Religion Among the Greeks and Romans—Lectures, 1912.* New York: Dover Publications, 1960.

Davies, N. *The Ancient Kingdoms of Mexico.* New York: Penguin Books, 1990.

Davis, W. "The Origins of Image Making." *Current Anthropology* 27 (1986): 193–216.

Davison, R. *Astrology.* New York: Arc Books, 1965.

Dean, G. "Forecasting Radio Quality by the Planets." *Skeptical Inquirer* 8 (Fall 1983): 48–56.

———. "Does Astrology Need to be True? Part 1: A Look at the Real Thing." *Skeptical Inquirer* 11 (Winter 86/87): 166–84.

———. "Does Astrology Need to be True? Part 2: The Answer Is No." *Skeptical Inquirer* 11 (Spring 1987): 257–73.

———. "Astrology Strikes Back, But to What Effect?" Review of *The Case for Astrology*, by John West. *Skeptical Inquirer* 18 (1993): 42–49.

Dean, G., and A. Mather. *Recent Advances in Natal Astrology: A Critical Review 1900–1976.* Rockport, Mass.: Para Research, 1977.

Dean, G., A. Mather, and I. Kelly. "Astrology." In *Encyclopedia of the Paranormal,* edited by Gordon Stein. Amherst, N.Y.: Prometheus Books, 1996.

Dean, G., I. Kelly, J. Rotton, and D. Saklofske. "The Guardian Astrology Study: A Critique and Reanalysis." *Skeptical Inquirer* 9 (Summer 1985): 327–38.

De Camp, L. *Great Cities of the Ancient World.* New York: Barnes & Noble, 1972.

Dicks, D. *Early Greek Astronomy to Aristotle.* Ithaca, N.Y.: Cornell University Press, 1970.

Dickson, D., and I. Kelly. "The 'Barnum Effect' in Personality Assessment: A Review of the Literature." *Psychological Reports* 57 (1985): 367–82.

Eisler, Robert. *The Royal Art of Astrology.* London: Herbert Joseph Ltd., 1946.

Ellis, M. "Observations on Mesopotamian Oracles and Prophetic Texts: Literary and Historiographic Considerations." *Journal of Cuneiform Studies* 41 (1989): 127–87.

Epictetus. *Discourses.* Chicago: Encyclopaedia Britannica, Inc., 1952.

Ertel, S. "Update on the 'Mars Effect.' " *Skeptical Inquirer* 16 (Winter 1992): 150–60.

Eysenck, H., and D. Nias. *Astrology: Science or Superstition?* New York: St. Martin's Press, 1982.

Farrington, Benjamin. *Greek Science.* London: C. Nichols & Co. Ltd., 1963.

Finkelstein, J. "Mesopotamian Historiography." *Proceedings of the American Philosophical Society* 107 (1963): 461–72.

Finley, M. *The Ancient Greeks.* New York: Penguin Books, 1991.

Fix, A. "Biorhythms and Sports Performance." *Zetetic* 1 (Fall/Winter 1976): 53–57.

French, C., et al. "Belief in Astrology: A Test of the Barnum Effect." *Skeptical Inquirer* 15 (Winter 1991): 166–72.

Gallo, E. "Synchronicity and the Archetypes." *Skeptical Inquirer* 18 (Summer 1994): 396–403.

Gardner, M. *Science: Good, Bad and Bogus.* Amherst, N.Y.: Prometheus Books, 1989.

Gauquelin, M. *The Cosmic Clocks.* Chicago: Henry Regnery Co., 1967.

———. *The Scientific Basis of Astrology.* New York: Stein & Day, 1969.

———. *Birthtimes: A Scientific Investigation of the Secrets of Astrology.* New York: Hill and Wang, 1983.

Gillispie, C., ed. *Dictionary of Scientific Biography.* New York: Scribners, 1978.

Gingerich, O. *The Eye of Heaven: Ptolemy, Copernicus, Kepler.* New York: American Institute of Physics, 1993.

Goodavage, J. *Astrology the Space Age Science.* West Nyack: Parker Publishing Company, Inc., 1966.

Grant, M. *From Alexander to Cleopatra.* New York: Charles Scribner's Sons, 1982.

———. *Greek and Roman Historians: Information and Misinformation.* London: Routledge, 1995.

Grayson, A., and Donald Redford. *Papyrus and Tablet.* Englewood Cliffs, N.J.: Prentice-Hall, Inc., 1973.

Hall, M. P. *The Story of Astrology.* New York: Philosophical Library, 1959.

Hammer, M. "A Recent Common Ancestry for Human Y Chromosomes." *Nature* 378 (1995): 376–78.

Hancock, G. *Fingerprints of the Gods.* New York: Crown Publishing, Inc., 1995.

Harcourt-Smith, Simon. *Babylonian Art.* New York: F. A. Stokes Co., 1928.

Harper, R., ed. *Assyrian and Babylonian Literature: Selected Translations.* New York: D. Appleton & Co., 1901.

Hawkins, G. S. "Astro-archaeology." *Smithsonian Institution Astrophysical Observatory* 226 (1966).

Heckert, H. *Lunationsrhythmen des menschlichen Organismus.* Leipzig: Akademischen Verlagsgesellschaft Geest & Portig, 1961.

Hines, T. "Biorhythm Theory: A Critical Review." *Skeptical Inquirer* 3 (Summer 1979): 26–36.

———. *Pseudoscience and the Paranormal.* Amherst, N.Y.: Prometheus Books, 1988.

Hinke, W. J. *Selected Babylonian Kudurru Inscriptions.* Leiden: E. J. Brill, 1911.

———. *A New Boundary Stone of Nebuchadnezzar I, from Nippur.* Philadelphia: University of Pennsylvania, 1907.

Hooke, S. H. *Babylonian and Assyrian Religion.* Norman: University Oklahoma Press, 1963.

Hoyrup, J. "Changing Trends in the Historiography of Mesopotamian Mathematics: An Insider's View." *History of Science* 34 (1996): 1–32.

Hunger, H. *Astrological Reports to Assyrian Kings.* Helsinki: Helsinki University Press, 1992.

Huxley, G. L. *The Interaction of Greek and Babylonian Astronomy.* Belfast: Queen's University, 1964.

Ianna, P., and C. Margolin. "Planetary Positions, Radio Propagation and the Work of J. H. Nelson." *Skeptical Inquirer* 6 (Fall 1981): 32–39.

Ianna, P., and C. Tolbert. "A Retest of Astrologer John McCall." *Skeptical Inquirer* 9 (Winter 84/85): 167–70.

Jacobsen, T. "Ancient Mesopotamian Religion: The Central Concerns." *Proceedings of the American Philosophical Society* 107 (1963): 473–84.

Jastrow, M. *The Religion of Babylonia and Assyria.* Boston: Ginn & Co., 1898.

———. *The Civilization of Babylonia and Assyria.* New York: J. B. Lippincott Co., 1915.

Jerome, L. "Astrology: Magic or Science?" *Humanist* 35 (1975): 10–16.

———. *Astrology Disproved.* Amherst, N.Y.: Prometheus Books, 1977.

Jones, A. "Ptolemy's First Commentator." *Transactions of the American Philosophical Society* 80 (1990): 1–61.

Kelly, I. "Astrology and Science: A Critical Examination." *Psychological Reports* 44 (1979): 1231–40.

Kelly, I., et al. "The Moon Was Full and Nothing Happened: A Review of Studies on the Moon and Human Behavior and Lunar Beliefs." *Skeptical Inquirer* 10 (Winter 1985/1986): 129–43.

Kelly, I., et al. "Astrology: A Critical Review." In *Philosophy of Science and the Occult*, edited by P. Grim. Albany: State University of New York Press, 1990.

Kelly, I., and R. Martens. "Lunar Phase and Birthdate: An Update." *Psychological Reports* 75 (1994): 507–11.

Kitto, H. *The Greeks*. Harmondsworth: Penguin Books Ltd., 1951.

Koch, W., and W. Knappich. *Horoskop and Himmelshaeuser*. Goeppingen/Fils, West Germany: Siriusverlag, 1959.

Kramer, S. *History Begins at Sumer*. London: Thomas and Hudson, 1961.

———. *Sumerian Mythology*. New York: Harper and Row, 1961.

———. "Cuneiform Studies and the History of Literature." *Proceedings of the American Philosophical Society* 107 (1963): 485–527.

———. *The Sumerians*. Chicago: University of Chicago Press, 1971.

Kroll, G., ed. *Vettii Valentis Anthologiarum Libri*. Zurich: Weidmann, 1973.

Krupp, E., ed. *In Search of Ancient Astronomies*. New York: Doubleday & Co., 1978.

Kurtz, P., and L. Nisbet. "Are Astronomers and Astrophysicists Qualified to Criticize Astrology?" *Zetetic* 1 (Fall/Winter 1976): 47–52.

Lackey, D. "A Controlled Test of Perceived Horoscope Accuracy." *Skeptical Inquirer* 6 (Fall 1981): 29–31.

Laesse, J. *People of Ancient Assyria*. New York: Barnes & Noble, 1963.

Leakey, R. *The Origin of Humankind*. New York: HarperCollins, 1994.

Legrain, L. *The Babylonian Collections of the University Museum*. Philadelphia: University Museum, 1944.

Lewinsohn, R. *Science, Prophecy and Prediction*. New York: Harper & Bros., 1961.

Lewis, J. *Astrology Encyclopedia*. Detroit: Visible Ink Press, 1994.

Ley, W. *Watchers of the Skies*. New York: Viking Press, 1966.

Lockyer, J. N. *The Dawn of Astronomy*. Cambridge, Mass.: MIT Press, 1964.

Lounsbury, F. "Maya Numeration, Computation and Calendrical Astronomy." In *Dictionary of Scientific Biography: Supplement*, edited by C. Gillispie. New York: Scribners, 1980.

McGervey, J. "A Statistical Test of Sun-Sign Astrology." *Zetetic* 1 (Spring/Summer 1977): 49–54.

McGillion, F. *The Opening Eye*. London: Coventure, 1980.

Margolix, E. *Sumerian Temple Documents*. New York: International Press, 1915.

Maringer, J. *The Gods of Prehistoric Man.* London: Weidenfeld and Nicolson, 1960.

Marshack, A. "Lunar Notation on Upper Paleolithic Remains." *Science* 146 (1964): 743–45.

Meissner, B. "Ueber Genethlialogie bei den Babyloniern." *KLIO* 19 (1925): 432–34.

Mills, D. *The Book of the Ancient Greeks.* New York: G. P. Putnam's Sons, 1925.

Nelson, J. "RCA Communication Paper." *New York Academy of Sciences* (April 1963).

Neugebauer, O. "The Rising Rimes in Babylonian Astronomy." *Journal of Cuneiform Studies* 7 (1953): 100–102.

———. *The Exact Sciences in Antiquity.* Providence, R.I.: Brown University Press, 1957.

———. "The Survival of Babylonian Methods in the Exact Sciences of Antiquity and Middle Ages." *Proceedings of the American Philosophical Society* 107 (1963): 528–35.

———. *A History of Ancient Mathematical Astronomy.* 3 volumes. New York: Springer-Verlag, 1975.

Neugebauer, O., and R. A. Parker. *Egyptian Astronomical Texts: Decans, Planets and Constellations,* vol 3. Providence, R.I.: Brown University Press, 1960.

Neugebauer, O., and H. Van Hoesen. *Greek Horoscopes.* Philadelphia: American Philosophical Society, 1959.

Newton, R. *The Crime of Claudius Ptolemy.* Baltimore, Md.: Johns Hopkins University Press, 1977.

Olmstead, A. T. *History of Assyria.* New York: Charles Scribner's Sons, 1923.

———. "Babylonian Astronomy—Historical Sketch." *American Journal of Semitic Languages and Literature* 55 (1948): 118–29.

Omarr, S. *My World of Astrology.* New York: Fleet Publishing Company, 1965.

O'Neil, W. *Early Astronomy from Babylonia to Copernicus.* Sydney: Sydney University Press, 1986.

Oppenheim, A. *Ancient Mesopotamia.* Chicago: University of Chicago Press, 1977.

———. "Man and Nature in Mesopotamian Civilization." In *Dictionary of Scientific Biography: Supplement,* edited by C. Gillispie. New York: Scribners, 1980.

Pannekock, A. *A History of Astronomy.* New York: Interscience Publishing, Inc., 1961.

Parker, R. *A Vienna Demotic Papyrus on Eclipse and Lunar Omina (Phenomena).* Providence, R.I.: Brown University Press, 1950.

———. "Egyptian Astronomy, Astrology and Calendrical Reckoning." In *Dictionary of Scientific Biography: Supplement,* edited by C. Gillispie. New York: Scribners, 1980.

Parrot, A. *Nineveh and Babylon.* Paris: Thames and Hudson, 1961.

Parry, R. *Astrology's Complete Book of Self-Defense.* Slough, UK: Quantum, 1990.

Pingree, D. "Dorotheus of Sidon." In *Dictionary of Scientific Biography: Supplement.* New York: Scribners, 1984.

Plotinus. *The Six Enneads.* Chicago: Encyclopaedia Britannica, Inc., 1952.

Plutarch. *The Lives of the Noble Grecians and Romans.* Chicago: Encyclopaedia Britannica, Inc., 1952.

Pokorny, A., and J. Jachimczyk. "The Questionable Relationship Between Homocides and the Lunar Cycle." *American Journal of Psychiatry* 121 (1964): 827–29.

Ptolemy, C. *The Almagest,* translated by R. Taliaferro. Chicago: Encyclopaedia Britannica, Inc., 1952.

———. *Tetrabiblos,* translated by F. Robbins. Cambridge, Mass.: Harvard University Press, 1964.

———. *The Almagest,* translated by G. Toomer. New York: Springer-Verlag, 1984.

———. *Tetrabiblos or Quadripartite—From the Greek Paraphrase of Proclus,* translated by J. Ashmand. Kila, Mont.: Kessinger Publishing Company, 1993.

Quincey, Paul. "The Strange Case of the New Haven Oysters." *Skeptical Inquirer* 17 (Winter 1993): 188–93.

Randi, J. *Flim-Flam!* Amherst, N.Y.: Prometheus Books, 1982.

Ravitz, L. J. "History, Measurement and Applicability of Periodic Changes in the Electromagnetic Field in Health and Disease." *Annals of the New York Academy of Sciences* (1960): 1144–1201.

Reinberg, A., and M. Smolensky. *Biological Rhythms and Medicine.* New York: Springer-Verlag, 1983.

Reiner, E., and D. Pingree. *Babylonian Planetary Omens: Enuma Anu Enlil.* Malibu: Undena Publishing, 1975.

Ringgren, H. *Religions of the Ancient Near East.* Philadelphia: Westminster Press, 1973.

Rodgers, J. *The Art of Astrology.* London: Herbert Jenkins, 1960.

Rotton, J. "Astrological Forecasts and the Commodity Market." *Skeptical Inquirer* 9 (Summer 1985): 339–46.

Roux, G. *Ancient Iraq.* Cleveland, Ohio: World Publishing Company, 1964.

Sachs, A. "Babylonian Horoscopes." *Journal of Cuneiform Studies* 6 (1952): 49–75.

———. "Sirius Dates in Babylonian Astronomical Texts of the Seleucid Period." *Journal of Cuneiform Studies* 6 (1952): 105–14.

———. *Late Babylonian Astronomical and Related Texts.* Providence, R.I.: Brown University Press, 1955.

Sarton, G. *A History of Science.* Cambridge, Mass.: Harvard University Press, 1960.

Scarre, C., ed. *Smithsonian Timelines of the Ancient World.* New York: Dorling Kindersley, 1993.

Seymour, P. *Astrology: The Evidence of Science.* New York: Viking Penguin, 1990.

Sileiko, V. [Schileico, W.]. "Mondlaufprognosen aus der Zeit der ersten babylonischen Dynastie." *Comptes Rendus de L'Academie des Sciences de l'Union des Republiques Sovietiques Socialistes* (1927): 125–28.

Sinnigen, W., and C. Robinson. *Ancient History: From Prehistoric Times to the Death of Justinian.* New York: MacMillan Publishing Company, 1981.

Startup, M. "The Origin of the Planetary Types." *Correlation* 2 (1981): 24–36.

Stein, G., ed. *Encyclopedia of the Paranormal.* Amherst, N.Y.: Prometheus Books, 1996.

Strabo. *Geography.* Cambridge, Mass.: Harvard University Press/Loeb Classical Library, 1932.

Tacitus, P. *The Annals and The Histories.* Chicago: Encyclopaedia Britannica, Inc., 1952.

Taub, L. *Ptolemy's Universe.* Chicago: Open Court Publishing Company, 1993.

Thierns, A. E. *Astrology in Mesopotamian Culture.* Leiden, Netherlands: E. J. Brill, 1935.

Thompson, R. C. *The Reports of the Magicians and Astrologers of Nineveh and Babylon.* London: Luzac and Company, 1900.

Time-Life Books, eds. *Cosmic Connections.* Alexandria, Va.: Time-Life Books, 1988.

Tomaschek, R. "Great Earthquakes and the Astronomical Positions of Uranus." *Nature* 184 (1959): 177–78.

Toomer, G. "Ptolemy." In *Dictionary of Scientific Biography,* edited by C. Gillispie. New York: Scribners, 1978.

———. "Hipparchus." In *Dictionary of Scientific Biography: Supplement,* edited by C. Gillispie. New York: Scribners, 1980.

Ucko, P., and A. Rosenfeld. *Palaeolithic Cave Art.* New York: McGraw-Hill Book Co., 1967.

Van der Waerden, B. L. "Babylonian Astronomy I. The Venus Tablets of Ammisaduqa." *Vooraziatische Philologie, Ex Oriente Lux.* Jaarbericht 10 (1948): 414–24.

———. "Babylonian Astronomy II. The Thirty-six Stars." *Journal of Near Eastern Studies* 8 (1949): 6–26.

———. "Babylonian Astronomy III. The Earliest Astronomical Computations." *Journal of Near Eastern Studies* 10 (1951): 20–34.

———. "History of the Zodiac." *Archiv fuer Orientforschung* 216 (1953): 216–30.

———. *Science Awakening II: The Birth of Astronomy.* New York: Oxford University Press, 1974.

Van Deusen, E. *Astrogenetics.* Garden City: Doubleday & Company, 1976.

Waddell, W. G., trans. *Manetho.* Cambridge, Mass.: Harvard University Press, 1964.

Weidner, E. F. "Ein Babylonishes Kompendium der Himmelskunde." *American Journal of Semitic Languages and Literature* 40 (1924).

———. "Die astrologische Serie Enuma Anu Enlil." *Archiv fuer Orientforschung* 14 (1942): 172–95.

West, J. *The Case for Astrology.* New York: Viking Penguin, 1991.

Westrum, R. "Scientists as Experts: Observations on 'Objections to Astrology.' " *Zetetic* 1 (Fall/Winter, 1976): 34–46.

Wheeler, A. "Biological Cycles and Rhythms vs. Biorhythms." *Skeptical Inquirer* 15 (Fall 1990): 75–82.

Whitehouse, R., ed. *The Facts on File Dictionary of Archaeology.* New York: Facts on File, Inc., 1983.

Whitehouse, R., and John Wilkins. *The Making of Civilization.* New York: Alfred Knopf, 1988.

Whittaker, E. *From Euclid to Eddington.* New York: Dover Publishing Inc., 1958.

Wilson, P. W. *Romance of the Calendar.* New York: W. W. Norton & Company, 1937.

Wood, B. "Origin and Evolution of the Genus Homo." *Nature* 355 (1992): 783–90.

Woolfolk, J. *The Only Astrology Book You'll Ever Need.* Lanham, Md.: First Scarborough House, 1990.

Index

Abell, G., 118
Albategnius, 113
Albumasar, 103
Alexandria, 83
Almagest, 90
Ammisaduqa, 29
An, 23
Andrews, E. J., 117
Aphrodite, 73
Apollo, 73
Apollonius, 75, 83
Aquarian Age, 127
Aquarius, 57
Ares, 73
Aries, 55–56
Aristarchus, 75, 83
Aristotle, 74
Assurbanipal, 34, 40
Assyrian era, 40
Astrolabes, 51

Atomism, 74
Aztecs, 114

Barnum Effect, 129–30
Baru-priest, 24–25
Bel-Marduk, 41
Berossus, 62, 111
Birth time, 122–24
Bok, B. J., 108
Boundary stone, 34

Calendar, 50–51
Cancer, 56
Capricorn, 57
Carneades, 80, 136
Casey, Caroline, 140
Cave art, 17
Celestial omens (Enuma Anu En-lil), 34, 43
Centaur, 19

Chaldeans, 61, 111
Chimera, 19
Cicero, 80–81, 111, 136
Circadian Rhythm, 116–17
Clay tablets, 33
Conception time, 122–24
Constellations, 55–59, 120
Correlation, 108–109
Critodemus, 75, 111
Cronus, 73
Culver, Roger B., 108, 118
Cuneiform script, 33
Cylinder seals, 21

Davison, Ronald, 138
Dean, G., 108–109, 119
Decans, 82
Diodorus, 111
Divination, 25
DNA, 17

Ea, 24
Early astrological text, 33
Elements (earth, air, fire, water),
    27, 74
Empedocles, 74
Enki, 23–24
Enlil, 23, 24, 59
Ennius, 79, 136
Enuma Anu Enlil (celestial omens),
    34, 43
Epictetus, 136
Epigenes, 75, 111
Eudoxus, 74–75, 136

Figulus, 80

Galen, 91

Gauquelin, Michel, 119, 131
Gemini, 56
Geocentric solar system, 90
Gnosticism, 84
Greek astrology, 75–76
Greenspan, B., 118

Hadrian, 82, 134
Hall, Manly, 111, 138
Hammurabi, 29
Hellenism, 72
Hellenistic astrology, 83–85
Hephaestion, 82, 102
Hermes, 73
Hermes Trismegistus, 75–76
Hines, T., 118
Hipparchus, 75, 83
Hittites, 29
Homo sapiens sapiens, 17, 112
Horoscopes, 63, 67, 69, 76, 85
Horoscopic astrology, 63, 75
Houses (zodiac), 113

Ianna, Philip A., 108
Inanna, 23, 24
Incas, 114
Ishtar, 24, 58, 59

Jarmo, 19
Jesus, 84
Jones, A., 133
Jove's animals, 80
Jung, Carl, 123
Jupiter, 58, 59

Ki, 23
Kiddinu, 62
Koine, 84

Kudurru, 34

Leo, 56
Libra, 57
Lists of stars (astrolabes), 51–52
Loci, 113
Lucretius, 136

Magi, 84
Marduk, 24, 58, 59
Mars, 58–59, 119–20
Mars Effect, 119–20
Maternus, 82
Mayans, 114
Mercury, 58, 59
Mesopotamia, 19
Mithraism, 84
Moon, 58, 59, 116–18
Muallafat, 19
mul.APIN, 52, 55
Museum (Alexandria), 83

Nabopolassar, 61
Nammu, 22
Nanna, 23, 24
Near East (ancient), 19
Nebo, 58, 59
Nelson, J. H., 119
Nergal, 58, 59
New Babylonian era, 61
Ninurta, 58, 59

Oldest horoscope, 63
Oliver, Ruth Hale, 112, 138
Omen reports, 33–34, 41–49, 130
Omens, 29, 43

Pappus, 103

Paul of Alexandria, 102
Petosiris/Nechepso, 75
Pisces, 57–58
Planets, 58–59, 118–20
Plato, 74
Plotinus, 137
Pokorny, A., 118
Porphyry, 102
Poseidonius, 76, 80
Praetorian Edict, 80
Precession of the equinoxes, 125
Proclus, 103
Ptolemy, 88–102
Pyramid, 114
Pythagorus, 73

Randi, James, 131–32
Ravitz, L. J., 117
Reliability, 109
Resonance, 118, 123
Righter, Carroll, 138
Robbins, F. E., 91, 133–34
Roman astrology, 79–83

Sagittarius, 57
Saros, 51
Saturn, 58, 59
Scorpio, 57
Selective memory, 131–32
Selene, 73
Serapis, 84
Sextus Empiricus, 82
Seymour, Percy, 118–19, 123
Shaman, 19
Shamash, 23, 24, 58
Sidereal astrology, 125–26
Sign (traditional) astrology, 126–27
Sin, 23, 24, 58

Sorcerer, 19
Stars, 110–21
Statistics, 108
Stetson, H. T., 117
Stoicism, 84
Strabo, 61
Sudines, 62–63
Sun, 58, 116–17
Sun signs, 135
Sunspots, 117
Symbols, 135

Taurus, 56
Temple system, 24–25
Tetrabiblos, 91–100
Theon, 103
Thompson, R. C., 43
Tides, 117
Tomaschek, Rudolf, 119
Tower of Babel, 25

Tucker, J., 123
Twins, 124

Utu, 23

Venus, 58–59, 118
Venus omens, 34
Vettius Valens, 85
Virgo, 56–57

Woolfolk, Joanna, 112

Yahweh, 84

Zeno, 62
Zeus, 73
Ziggurat, 25
Zodiac, 50, 52, 63, 67
Zodiacal constellations, 55–58